Table of Contents

To the great 19th and 20th century walker,
Edward Payson Weston,
who inspired many children with handshakes
on his walks across America.

PART ONE

A Teacher's Guide to Walking Wellness

Walking Wellness is a 4th to 8th grade curriculum taught by Health and Physical Education specialists and classroom teachers. The curriculum consists of 16 hands-on workshops focusing on different aspects of Fitness Walking, Cardiovascular Conditioning, Nutrition & Weight Control, Walking Techniques & Posture, Stress Control, Tobacco-free Living and Lifestyle Planning.

The primary focus is on *experiential learning, self-improvement* and *non-competitive walking exercises* that **all** students can do, regardless of their athletic abilities.

This book is your *teaching guide* for this course. Over the next 43 pages, each Walking Wellness workshop is explained—from the workshop objectives to the teacher's lesson plans, to the accompanying homework assignments and answers.

As you teach **Walking Wellness**, students follow along in their own workbooks (see Part Two of this book). They are responsible for recording their own personal data and experiences for each workshop. This involves determining heart rates, walking speeds, caloric intakes and walking energy expenditures, walking posture analysis and walking-lifestyle action plans. Each workshop has a reinforcing homework assignment.

To teach **Walking Wellness**, you do not need a specialist degree in exercise physiology or physical education. You will however, need to read all sections of this teacher's resource guide thoroughly—especially the Teacher's Lesson Plan (Section III). In addition, it is recommended that you attend either a 1/2-day or full day **Walking Wellness Teacher's Training Seminar*** to learn how to conduct the most effective and motivational workshops for your students.

Once you start teaching **Walking Wellness**, your attitude toward Health and Physical Education may change. Specifically, you may realize that:

1. Physical Education can have accountability.
2. Health and Physical Education can be taught as an integrated curriculum.
3. Math, science, and language arts can also be integrated into a wellness curriculum.
4. All students can be winners in a walking program.
5. Walking improves a child's attitude toward wellness.

Now as you move ahead into your **Walking Wellness** units, take our best wishes for a healthy, happy teaching experience. And have a great year of walking.

*For more information on **Walking Wellness Teacher Training** for school districts, contact:

Creative Walking, Inc.
P.O. Box 50296
St. Louis, MO 63105
314-721-3600

Fort River Elementary School Walkers (Amherst, MA)

By walking 10 extra minutes a day, the average child burns up an additional 10,000 calories of stored fat per year. This can translate to 3 pounds less body fat come summertime.

I

Why Children Should Walk

Why Should Children Walk?

The average American child watches 25 hours of TV weekly, rides a school bus, lives on a high-fat diet, and lacks motivation to exercise regularly.

Most school programs include a component of jogging, which while OK for some, is disliked by many. The problem is that jogging (or running) can cause leg muscle tightening, sore feet and nasty "side stitches" in the rib cage. Let's face it, for many jogging is no fun. Besides, jogging and other sweat-producing activities have children spending much of their PE time in the locker room changing clothes, showering and fixing their hair.

Walking is *one* exercise students can do free of pain, injury, and sweat—without wasting ¼ of the gym period in the locker room. Walking proves the "No Pain, No Gain" theory of exercise wrong. Plus walking controls aggression, stress and body weight. Walking promotes self-esteem and creative thinking while strengthening the heart. Twenty minutes a day of walking (in place of TV) lets a child burn about 25,000 additional calories per year. That alone (without dieting) will burn up to 7 extra pounds of fat!

At the Fort River Elementary School students start the *Aerobic Walking Workshop* by pacing at 3½ mph (a 17-minute mile). This pace is fast enough to bring 3 out of every 4 students into the aerobic target zone for good cardiovascular conditioning.

Twenty Reasons Why Children Should Walk

Walking. . .

develops a good wellness attitude
develops good posture

stabilizes friendships
stabilizes blood pressure

encourages use of senses
encourages drug-free living

promotes language development
promotes physical coordination

lets everyone participate
lets everyone have fun

builds self-esteem
builds strong bones

increases attentiveness
increases muscle mass

controls disruptive behavior
controls fat cell growth

diminishes stress
diminishes hyperactivity

strengthens communications
strengthens the heart

Walking is our safest, most sensible lifetime exercise, and it's perfect for school children. For them it's fun. It's physical yet inexpensive, and it's teachable. Unlike baseball, tennis, bowling, swimming and gymnastics, walking requires no special facilities. Unlike the contact sports, walking is injury free. Unlike wrestling, football, or basketball, walking favors neither sex. Unlike any other physical education program, a creative walking curriculum can enhance reading, writing, and analytical skills. These are the goals of *Walking Wellness*—an integrated wellness curriculum dealing with: (1) cardiovascular health, (2) aerobic fitness, (3) energy and food calories, (4) weight control and diet, (5) stress reduction, (6) communications, (7) teamwork, and (8) lifestyle planning.

Footnote: Brisk walking burns about the same number of calories mile for mile as jogging—but without the high impact stress placed on the joints as in jogging. Walking, with ⅓ the impact landing of jogging, creates just the right amount of stress to help bone growth and muscle-skeleton formation.

Why Teachers Should Walk

In the space provided below, list reasons why you should walk BEFORE, DURING or AFTER school hours.

Benefits of walking BEFORE school

_____
_____
_____
_____
_____

Benefits of LUNCHTIME walking

_____
_____
_____
_____
_____

Benefits of walking AFTER school

_____
_____
_____
_____
_____
_____

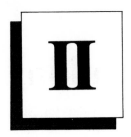

Creative Walking Education

Walking Wellness is a creative educational course consisting of 16 walking workshops. The workshops exercise children's minds as well as their bodies. Just about every subject is touched, from the principles of aerobics and nutrition to such basic skills as reading, writing, and analytical thinking. Healthy lifestyle is the bottom line.

The 16 *Walking Wellness* workshops fit into regular periods of class instruction. By covering one workshop every 1 to 2 weeks, you can use *Walking Wellness* as a year-long instructional tool.

During each lesson, students walk, talk, write, read, reason, calculate, plan, analyze, cooperate, and discover. Every minute is a learning experience, whether the class is in motion, or thinking about that motion. Roughly half the course is physical walking exercise; the other half is "walking for the mind." No workshop is complete without homework. These assignments often ask family members to participate in lifestyle planning. By the last workshop students begin writing their own *WALKING ACTION PLANS.*

Teaching Objectives

The main objectives of *Walking Wellness* are to:

1. teach students lifelong aerobic walking in a non-competitive, win-win environment.

2. use walking as a medium to support reading, writing, math, and science.

3. have walking support healthy lifestyle in workshops where students think about and discuss stress, tobacco, and nutrition while walking.

4. encourage teamwork, group communication, respect, and honesty in real-life, fun walks.

5. involve family members in walking workshops and lifestyle planning.

6. have students develop realistic *Walking Action Plans* that make walking a lasting habit.

At the Oaklea Middle School, the first school in America to pilot *Walking Wellness,* children start on a "Straw Walk" (workshop 3). Here students walk briskly on a measured loop collecting "straws" each time they complete a lap. By the end of the Straw Walk students have: (1) learned about aerobic pacing, (2) measured their walking heart rates, (3) calculated their walking speeds, (4) measured their baseline fitness levels, (5) recorded their physical data, and (6) received 15 minutes of good aerobic exercise—all in one workshop. Note: Only 5 percent of our nation's youth can walk 5+ MPH (5 straws collected for 15 consecutive minutes)! What's your walking pace?

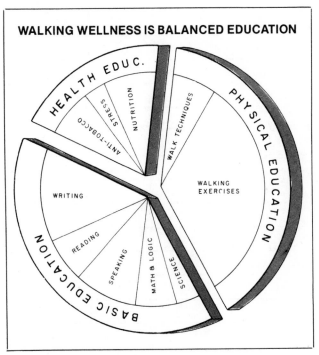

WALKING WELLNESS IS BALANCED EDUCATION

HEALTH EDUC.
ANTI-TOBACCO
STRESS
NUTRITION
WALK TECHNIQUES
PHYSICAL EDUCATION
WALKING EXERCISES
WRITING
READING
SPEAKING
MATH & LOGIC
SCIENCE
BASIC EDUCATION

Creative Walking Education

In the space provided below, list all of your creative ideas for using "walking" as an educational tool. Suggestion: Try composing your list on a fresh-air walk.

Academic— Walking Projects & Lessons

_____

_____

_____

_____

_____

Fitness— Health Projects

_____

_____

_____

_____

_____

Homeroom— Recess— Lunchtime Activities

_____

_____

_____

_____

_____

Extracurricular Projects— Intramurals

_____

_____

_____

_____

_____

_____

_____

The Teacher's Lesson Plan

Teaching these 16 workshops is an educational experience for you as well as your students. You will learn how a child perceives walking and the manner in which a child thinks while he or she is on a walk. The workshops "move" extremely fast, exercise after exercise, and sometimes you will wonder how the period could have ended so fast. That can be a problem especially if you have not yet had a chance to summarize your lesson and explain the homework. For these reasons a *Teacher's Lesson Plan* is included for each of the 16 workshops. These lesson plans explain the workshop objectives, logistics, and teacher preparations required. Potential problems are discussed and suggestions are offered on how to improve workshop effectiveness. The key points for lesson closure are also outlined with the homework concepts and answers.

Flexible Scheduling of Workshops

It's a drizzly, gray morning. You were going to take your class out for a *Walking Wellness* workshop. You say, "Forget it!" But what are your alternatives? How about waiting several days for blue skies? The delay should not affect your overall schedule as long as you average a few workshops per month. At this rate, the entire curriculum can be completed in 1 school year. In fact, spreading out the workshops allows time for homework and reinforcement exercises. Holidays are no problem either. Say you completed Workshop 8 before Christmas recess; simply kick off the new year with Workshop 9. After that, just continue conducting workshops to fit your teaching schedule.

WORKSHOP 1

A Walking Field Trip

1. Objectives
2. The Workshop Plan
3. Teacher Preparation
4. Conducting the Workshop
5. Potential Pitfalls
6. Suggestions
7. Lesson Closure
8. The Homework

Living Within a ½-Hour Class Period

Most of the *Walking Wellness* workshops can be taught in the time frame of a 30 to 40 minute class. If your classes run somewhat longer, that is even better. The key lies in proportioning your time well and getting off to a prompt start. However, do not get upset if some of your workshops tend to overrun the first time around.

In most workshops students will not need to perform extensive locker room changes (other than dropping off their books and making a quick outer clothing adjustment). Gym shorts and T-shirts are necessary only in warmer weather. Showers after the workshops should rarely be required either inasmuch as most of the workshops deal in no-sweat, easy-gaited walking.

Overall you will find that most workshops are designed with 15 to 20 minutes of walking and 10 to 15 minutes of discussion and lesson summary. This amounts to about 60 percent active component and 40 percent reading, writing and group discussion.

Teacher's Notes

My Teaching Objectives _____
_____
_____
_____
_____
_____
_____
_____

My Walking Wellness Implementation Plan _____
_____
_____
_____
_____
_____
_____
_____

My Scheduling Plan _____
_____
_____
_____
_____
_____
_____
_____

My Teaching Ideas _____
_____
_____
_____
_____
_____
_____
_____

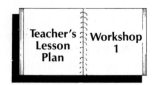

Teacher's Lesson Plan | Workshop 1

A Walking Field Trip

1 Objectives

A. to convey a positive image of walking to students
B. to show students they are capable of going places on foot
C. to improve students' awareness of community and environment
D. to gain an appreciation for walking

2 The Workshop Plan

In the time frame of *one* regular period, you and your class will visit any nearby "site of interest" on foot and return to school for a brief discussion of that Walking Field Trip.

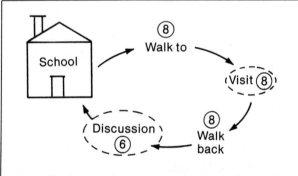

Note: Circled numbers represent approximate time (in minutes) for each segment of workshop.

3 Teacher Preparation

A. It helps to have selected the *site* in advance so that the *host* at the receiving end is aware of and willing to receive your class.
B. Parent consents may be required.
C. A teacher's aid is recommended for student supervision.
D. The path should be measured to ensure it is no longer than a ½-mile walk.

4 Conducting the Workshop

There are 5 basic steps in this workshop:

1. assemble class
2. departure
3. site visit
4. return to school
5. postwalk note-taking and discussion

5 Potential Pitfalls

The most common pitfall is returning to school too late for your discussion and lesson wrap-up. However, the most serious pitfall is "horseplay" that might lead to an accident.

6 Suggestions

A. Could your students vote democratically on where they'd like to visit?
B. Could you enlist parents or other staff to join you on the trip?
C. Could you get clearance to use a double-period to expand this workshop into an hour field trip?

7 Lesson Closure

The most important concept to reiterate is the feeling that comes from going somewhere on foot—the pride, the accomplishment, the physical sensation, the self-esteem, and the realization that "we are not slaves to the automobile."

8 The Homework

To build on the positive feelings and momentum of this Field Trip, students are asked to seriously consider those places that they'd be willing to walk to instead of riding.

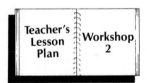

Teacher's Lesson Plan | Workshop 2

Aerobic Walking

1 Objectives

A. to have students discover for themselves the proper walking pace that *"pushes"* their heart rate into the *aerobic target zone*
B. to teach students the relationship between *walking pace* and *exercise heart rate*
C. to introduce students to varying degrees of "moderate" to "brisk" walking

2 The Workshop Plan

In classic trial and error fashion, students will have *3* attempts to "zero-in" on their own *Aerobic Walking Pace*. As teacher, you will lead your class in the opening 3.5 MPH lap (¼ mile in 4 minutes, 17 seconds). After that lap, students will select their own pace for the remaining 2 trials (Trials 2 and 3) and measure their heart rates for those 2 trial walks to see if they have reached the *aerobic training zone*.

3 Teacher Preparation

A. The very first action you need to take is to design and build your own *Straw Walk course*. Do not get scared. Building a Straw Walk course is simple, inexpensive, and fun. It takes less than an hour for 2 people as described below.

Designing and Building Your Own Straw Walk Course

Pick a spot. Look for a wide open flat area with a smooth walking surface that is away from traffic. If you already have access to a ¼-mile track on or adjacent to your school grounds, your biggest problem is solved. If not, pick out the best open area. *Avoid* a walking loop in which students can walk out of view (that is, around and behind a building). This may lead to the temptation of cheating (running) when out of the teacher's sight.

Measure and mark the course. An easy way to measure your Straw Walk course is to mark off 44-yard segments with a long construction tape measure or a 44-yard long string marked with 2 knots. When you close in on the last 44-yard segment it should measure 42 to 46 yards. If that last section measures *less than* 42 yards, you will need to expand the overall middle of your Straw Walk course. Similarly, if the last section measures more than 46 yards, you will need to shrink the course a bit.

For an ideal Straw Walk loop, avoid sharp turns, bumpy ground, and hilly terrain. Try to pick a well-drained surface. If you use an existing ¼-mile track, you still need to lay out tenth markers. *Note:* Your markers should be removable. However, you should still mark the ground with some permanent, visible land-mark to facilitate reconstruction of your Straw Walk course. If at all possible, keep your Straw Walk course as permanent as possible. This way everyone (staff and students) can practice on it anytime!

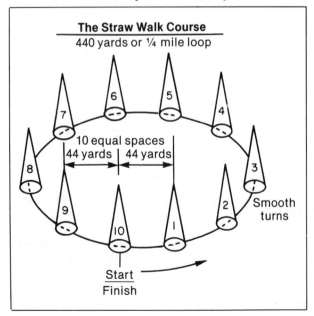

The Straw Walk Course
440 yards or ¼ mile loop

10 equal spaces
44 yards | 44 yards

Smooth turns

Start
Finish

B. As teacher you need to become proficient at walking 3.5 MPH by practicing some easy walking laps of the Straw Walk course. Try to complete your laps between 4:10 and 4:25 (min:sec). A perfect 3.5 MPH lap is 4:17. With a little practice, you'll be hitting your 4:15 to 4:20 laps right on time!

4 Conducting the Workshop

The first lap is easy because everyone finishes at the same time. Thus it's easy to lead your students in a 6-second pulse check all at once. However in Trials 2 and 3, each student will be finishing his or her lap at their own pace. So in these cases you will need to be conducting quick pulse checks in succession as groups of students finish their laps.

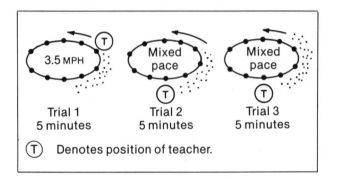

3.5 MPH

Trial 1
5 minutes

Mixed pace

Trial 2
5 minutes

Mixed pace

Trial 3
5 minutes

T Denotes position of teacher.

5 Potential Pitfalls

Without tight overseeing, students finishing their laps will forget to take their pulses *immediately* after the lap. This destroys the accuracy of the *exercise heart rate*, (due to *heart rate recovery*). So as your students finish, get their attention and conduct a quick pulse check.

6 Suggestions

A simple *pulse check* can be administered by asking your students to place their 2nd or 3rd fingers *gently* on their carotid arteries (groove in the right-front side of neck) so as *not* to stop the blood flow to the brain. *You*, as teacher, give a *start* and *stop* signal for the 6-second pulse count. After this count, explain that all the students need to do is multiply their count by 10 (or add "0" to their count) for finding their *walking heart rates* (beats per minute).

7 Lesson Closure

After each trial, but especially at the very end, ask your students to divide into *3* groups depending on what *walking heart rate* they achieved. The 3 groups are:

Less than 120 BPM
(11 or less beats
in 6 seconds)

Group 1 (too slow)

Between 120 and 150 BPM
(12 to 15 beats in 6 seconds)

Group 2 (aerobic)

More than 150 BPM
(16 or more beats
in 6 seconds)

Group 3 (too fast)

Explain to groups 1 and 3 that by speeding up (group 1) or slowing down (group 3), they would be working their bodies in the *aerobic target zone* for ideal cardiovascular conditioning.

8 Homework

Students are to check their pulses for various activities outside of class and to figure out which of those activities raise their heart rates to the *aerobic training zone*.

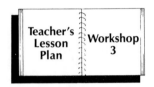

The Straw Walk

1 Objectives

A. to establish a fitness baseline measurement for each student based on how far a child can walk in 15 minutes

B. to demonstrate the true meaning of steady aerobic pacing

C. to let students discover their own *maximum walking speed* in miles per hour as a basis for future self-improvement

D. to show children that under maximum effort conditions, walking is a challenging exercise

E. to provide children with 15 minutes of safe aerobic walking exercise at a sustained elevated heart rate

2 The Workshop Plan

After an easy warm-up walking lap, challenge your students to walk as fast as they can around the *Straw Walk* course for 15 straight minutes. Each time they complete a lap, you will hand them a straw. After 15 minutes, your whistle will signal them to stop immediately. Then blow 2 more consecutive whistles (6 seconds apart) so students can check their pulse. At this point, you will circle the track asking students to announce their scores to you. Check their accuracy. Each student then falls in behind you to walk along for a partial cool-down.

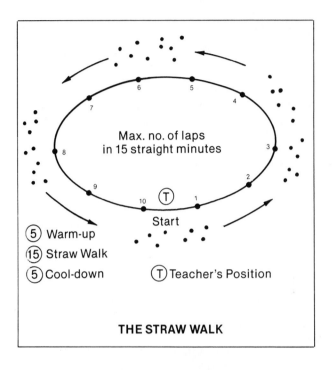

Max. no. of laps
in 15 straight minutes

Start

(5) Warm-up
(15) Straw Walk
(5) Cool-down

(T) Teacher's Position

THE STRAW WALK

3 Teacher Preparation

Most critical: You must have your Straw Walk course accurately *measured* and *marked* with *ten orange cones* (or any highly visible markers) spread 44 yards apart (440 yards or ¼ mile loop) along your walking loop. The markers need to be clearly marked "1," "2," . . . "9," so that students will be able to quickly determine the fraction of their last lap completed when the 15-minute whistle blows.

Once your Straw Walk course is in order (by the way, it needs to be built in time for Workshop 2), all you will need is a *whistle*, a *stop watch*, your *teacher's workbook*, and about *150 straws* (5 straws per student to be safe, although most students will achieve only 4 + Straw Walk scores).

To get the "hang" of the Straw Walk routine, go out on the Straw Walk course by yourself or with a few staff members and perform a "dry run" (actually a "dry walk") during which you will hand out straws to your walkers.

4 Conducting the Workshop

Think of the Straw Walk as a 4-stage workshop: (1) opening warm-up walk (1 lap), (2) maximal performance walk (15 minutes), (3) score keeping and cool-down lap, and (4) lesson closure. Time will be at a premium so move quickly through these 4 *stages*.

5 Potential Pitfalls

There are 5 major *pitfalls* that can destroy the accuracy of any Straw Walk score:

1. If a child runs, that is in effect cheating. You can give that child a one time warning or disqualify that child immediately.

2. If a child slows down to collect his or her straw, that hurts their performance. Hand the students their straws in full stride even if it means keeping pace with them a few steps. *One Person (you)* should hand out straws. When 2 people get involved, things get too confusing.

3. If the Straw Walk course is inaccurately measured, you are distorting the results of this walk and all workshops that follow. *Recommendation:* Have several other staff members certify the course. (Shoot for 440 yards plus or minus 5 yards.)

4. If students enter the infield of the Straw Walk course that is cheating.

5. If students "lounge" in social conversation at the back of the pack they will not be achieving a *maximal effort score*. Keep encouraging them to move quickly.

6 Suggestions

A mistake students often make is walking *too* fast on their first Straw Walk lap. To slow the students down at the start, tell them that: (1) "this is *not* a race," and (2) "Remember you need to walk fast for 15 full minutes, so don't use all of your energy on the opening lap."

Be ready for the lead group of students when they come in for their 1st straws. They will be finishing their 1st lap in about 3 minutes. Be alert at all times, but especially when 3, 4, or 5 students come by in a group. If necessary hand the students straws while you walk with them so as not to slow them down. Separate the social talkers, and do not lose track of time as the 15-minute mark approaches.

7 Lesson Closure

Summarize the objectives of the Straw Walk by emphasizing 3 points:

1. The Straw Walk is a measure of your Aerobic Fitness.

2. Because a ¼ of an hour walk on a ¼-mile walking loop equates mathematically to a 1-hour walk on a 1-mile walking loop, your Straw Walk score also represents your *walking speed* in MILES PER HOUR.

3. By practicing your walking, living healthier, and becoming more fit, you can *improve your Straw Walk score*.

Conducting Follow-Up Straw Walks

Some teachers take their classes through as many as a dozen or more straw walks a year because they realize that this is one of the best 15-minute aerobic exercises for their children.

By doing such repeated Straw Walks, children do learn to pace better. Multiple Straw Walks also give them opportunities to keep breaking their own personal records.

On page 12 in the Student Workbook, children are given second opportunity to improve their Straw Walk performances. Before you kick-off their second Straw Walk, take a few moments to review the LOW and HIGH performance factors (see page 12 of the Student Workbook) with your class. Ask your students which factors they think are most critical to good Straw Walk performances.

Straw Walk Mathematics

A most valuable resource chart is provided on page 13 in the Student Workbook. This chart is titled STRAW WALK MATHEMATICS, and it tells the student how to compute a Straw Walk Score.

For example, by adding the number of straws you collected during the Straw Walk (COLUMN 1) to the fraction of the last lap you completed (COLUMN 2), you will find your STRAW WALK SCORE under COLUMN 3. This chart also provides the equivalent MPH pace (COLUMN 4) for each Straw Walk Score. You can also determine your equivalent time for walking ¼ mile (COLUMN 5) or 1 mile (COLUMN 6) for any given Straw Score.

Straw Walk Mathematics

Converting Your *Straw Walk* Score to *Lap Time*

To calculate your *Straw Walk* score, *add* together the number of straws you collected in 15 minutes (Column 1) *and* the fraction of the last lap you completed (Column 2). The sum is your *Straw Walk* score (Column 3) which also tells you your average walking speed (Column 4) in *miles per hour*. Columns 5 & 6 tell you *how long* it would take you to walk ¼ mile and 1 mile, respectively.

(Column 1) No. Straws In Hand	(Column 2) The Tenth Marker Closest To Where You Finished	(Column 3) Straw Walk Score	(Column 4) Average Walking Speed	(Column 5) ¼ Mi. Time (1 Lap) (min:sec)	(Column 6) 1 Mi. Time (4 Laps) (min:sec)
3 Straws	0/10	3.0	3.0 MPH	5:00	20:00
3 Straws	1/10	3.1	3.1 MPH	4:50	19:20
3 Straws	2/10	3.2	3.2 MPH	4:41	18:45
3 Straws	3/10	3.3	3.3 MPH	4:32	18:10
3 Straws	4/10	3.4	3.4 MPH	4:25	17:40
3 Straws	5/10	3.5	3.5 MPH	4:17	17:08
3 Straws	6/10	3.6	3.6 MPH	4:10	16:40
3 Straws	7/10	3.7	3.7 MPH	4:03	16:12
3 Straws	8/10	3.8	3.8 MPH	3:56	15:46
3 Straws	9/10	3.9	3.9 MPH	3:50	15:22
4 Straws	0/10	4.0	4.0 MPH	3:45	15:00
4 Straws	1/10	4.1	4.1 MPH	3:40	14:38
4 Straws	2/10	4.2	4.2 MPH	3:34	14:16
4 Straws	3/10	4.3	4.3 MPH	3:29	13:57
4 Straws	4/10	4.4	4.4 MPH	3:24	13:37
4 Straws	5/10	4.5	4.5 MPH	3:20	13:20
4 Straws	6/10	4.6	4.6 MPH	3:15	13:02
4 Straws	7/10	4.7	4.7 MPH	3:12	12:45
4 Straws	8/10	4.8	4.8 MPH	3:07	12:30
4 Straws	9/10	4.9	4.9 MPH	3:03	12:15
5 Straws	0/10	5.0	5.0 MPH	3:00	12:00
5 Straws	1/10	5.1	5.1 MPH	2:56	11:45
5 Straws	2/10	5.2	5.2 MPH	2:53	11:32
5 Straws	3/10	5.3	5.3 MPH	2:50	11:20
5 Straws	4/10	5.4	5.4 MPH	2:46	11:07
5 Straws	5/10	5.5	5.5 MPH	2:43	10:55
5 Straws	6/10	5.6	5.6 MPH	2:40	10:42
5 Straws	7/10	5.7	5.7 MPH	2:38	10:32
5 Straws	8/10	5.8	5.8 MPH	2:35	10:20
5 Straws	9/10	5.9	5.9 MPH	2:32	10:10
6 Straws	0/10	6.0	6.0 MPH	2:30	10:00

EXAMPLE:
Johnny winds up with 4 straws in his hand as he stands alongside the 7th cone of the Straw Walk Course when your whistle sounds signifying the end of the Straw Walk.

QUESTION: How can Johnny use his Straw Walk Math Tables in his workbook to find out his pace?

ANSWER: By turning to page 13, Johnny can first look up his Straw Walk Score by placing a ruler or straight edge horizontally across the one line that shows 4 Straws and 7/10's of a marker. COLUMN 3 gives him his Straw Walk Score (4.7) and COLUMN 4 tells Johnny that he averaged 4.7 MPH for a full 15 minutes. By moving horizontally across the chart, Johnny will also note that he is capable of walking one lap of a 1/4 mile track in 3 minutes and 12 seconds (COLUMN 5). Under COLUMN 6, Johnny finds his mile time to be 12 minutes and 45 seconds!

8 Homework

This homework assignment is essential to the whole *Walking Wellness* course. Students will need to refer back to this assignment throughout their final workshops.

The Workshop 3 Homework helps students plan for self-improvement—and specifically it helps them strive for improved Straw Walk Scores. It is recommended that this assignment be attempted AFTER students have completed TWO Straw Walks. This will permit them to compare their own Straw Walk performances and set personal goals for the future.

Teacher's Notes on the Straw Walk

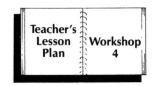
The 3.5 MPH Teamwalk

1 Objectives

A. to show students the value of *teamwork* and *good communication skills* in a *democratic environment*

B. to teach students the value of 3.5 MPH walking

C. to have students train themselves to walk at a 3.5 MPH pace

2 The Workshop Plan

After dividing your class up into 5 teams (Red, Yellow, Orange, Green, Blue), you will start one team every 2 minutes, on the minute, and in sequential order: Red team at 0:00, Orange at 2:00, Yellow at 4:00, etc. As a team returns, you will call out their *lap time* and have them huddle among themselves to discuss their performance. After all teams have completed their second laps, conduct an open discussion on *team performance*.

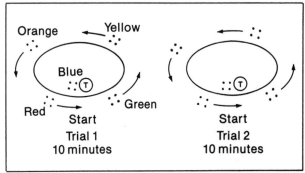

3 Teacher Preparation

Obviously this workshop must take place on the calibrated Straw Walk course. All you need is your *workbook, stop watch,* and your *color card deck.* To save time at the beginning of your workshop, shuffle your deck and quickly deal out cards to your students. Have all your teams take their positions as shown on page 16 of the Student Workbook.

4 Conducting the Workshop

Teamwalk Sequence Chart

	Start Time	Finish Time	Lap Time
RED	0:00	___:___	___:___
ORANGE	2:00	___:___	___:___
YELLOW	4:00	___:___	___:___
GREEN	6:00	___:___	___:___
BLUE	8:00	___:___	___:___
RED (2nd Lap)	10:00	___:___	___:___
ORANGE (2nd Lap)	12:00	___:___	___:___
YELLOW (2nd Lap)	14:00	___:___	___:___
GREEN (2nd Lap)	16:00	___:___	___:___
BLUE (2nd Lap)	18:00	___:___	___:___

5 Potential Pitfalls

In the *Teamwalk* it is essential that you *start* your teams on time (on the minute) and *stop* them at their finish (for their final lap time). Simultaneously, you need to keep bringing the next team up on the on-deck circle in preparation for their walk. To help you keep track of everyone, follow the *sequence chart* above.

Student warning: Emphasize to each team that they absolutely must stick together as a "tight" unit in close conversation.

6 Suggestions

A. Try to place 4 to 5 students on a team. That makes for a good walking conversational circle (see diagram below). Be sure each team consists of as equal a number of students as possible.

Best Walking Configurations

Team of 4	Team of 5	Team of 6
X X	X X	X X
X X	X	X X
	X X	X X
2 up, 2 back	2 up, 3 back	3 up, 3 back

B. Encourage all teammates to *talk, listen,* and *compromise* with each other when there is disagreement as to what speed to walk.

C. Make sure all students write down their *start times* and their *finish times,* and that they calculate their *lap times.*

D. To avoid temptation, make sure all students wearing wrist watches remove those time pieces for the length of this workshop.

E. As each team stands on deck, ask them how they feel about the teamwork process. Are they functioning as a team or independently?

7 Lesson Closure

Some good questions to ask your class *before* adjourning:

A. How many of you now know how to walk 3.5 MPH?

B. How many of you think you've learned something about the importance of group communications, teamwork, and listening to others?

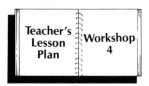

The 4.0 MPH Teamwalk

1 Objectives

A. to reinforce *teamwork* and *good communication skills*

B. to have students train themselves to walk a 4.0 MPH pace.

2 The Workshop Plan

This 4.0 MPH Teamwalk exercise is nearly identical to the previous *Teamwalk,* except the pace has been increased from 3.5 to 4.0 MPH. As before, start each team every 2 minutes, on the minute.

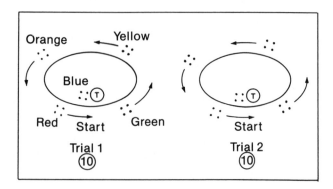

3 Teacher Preparation

Prepare the same way as for the 3.5 MPH Teamwalk. There is no need to compose new teams unless for some reason you choose to do so. To save time, have your students regroup with their previous Red, Orange, Yellow, Green, and Blue teammates. *Note:* New team assignments will be made in all future workshops, except in the case of Workshops 10 and 11 (2-part workshop) where we want to hold the *team unit* together.

4 Conducting the Workshop

Follow the same format as in the 3.5 MPH Teamwalk.

5 Potential Pitfalls

A new potential pitfall is introduced into the 4.0 MPH *Teamwalk* in that certain students may have trouble physically keeping pace at 4 MPH. What should a team do if 1 or 2 students agree on the 4 MPH pace but can't physically keep pace with the group? *Answer:* Students who really can't maintain a 4.0 MPH pace should ease up and walk at their fastest reasonable pace. At the end of their lap, they should rejoin their teammates.

6 Suggestions

Follow the general "teamwalk" guidelines, however this time have your students pay attention to: (1) any improvements in their teamwork and good communication skills, and (2) the physical differences between 3.5 and 4.0 MPH walking.

7 Lesson Closure

A few key questions to ask your students:

A. Was it easier to walk as a team at 3.5 MPH or 4.0 MPH? Why?
B. What improvements have you noticed in your teamwork and good communication skills since Workshop 4?
C. How would you describe the differences between 3.5 MPH and 4.0 MPH walking?
D. How many of you think you could now walk a 15-minute mile, plus or minus 5 seconds, without looking at your watches?

8 Homework

The homework assignment consists of answering 7 very basic questions reinforcing the principles of the *Teamwalk Workshop.*

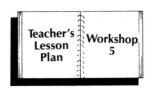

Walking in Rhythm

1 Objectives

A. to show students that by swinging their arms properly they can walk faster and for longer distances without tiring
B. to quantify the specific performance differences between a *no arm swing walk*, an *easy arm swing walk*, and a *high-energy arm swing walk*

2 The Workshop Plan

In workshop 5 your students will perform 3 separate ¼-mile walks on the Straw Walk course: Walk 1, arm swing is *not* permitted; Walk 2, students are to swing their arms *naturally* and *comfortably* at their sides; Walk 3, students should really pump and thrust their arms like a powerful locomotive. For all 3 walks, you as teacher are to call out their lap times as they finish their ¼ mile. All students should immediately record their times on page 21 of their workbooks. *Note:* Start your entire class as 1 whole unit.

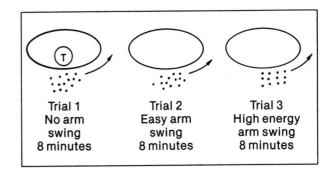

| Trial 1 | Trial 2 | Trial 3 |
| No arm swing 8 minutes | Easy arm swing 8 minutes | High energy arm swing 8 minutes |

3 Teacher Preparation

Bring your *teacher's workbook* and a *stop watch* to Workshop 5. *Note:* To become familiar with the effects of arm-swing, you might practice walks 1, 2, and 3 in Workshop 5 before teaching your first class.

4 Conducting the Workshop

In Workshop 5 you will not be pressured for time compared to most other workshop lessons. Thus you can conduct open discussions between each of the walks so that students can share their feelings of how arm swing contributes to walking performance.

5 Potential Pitfalls

To get the best indication of how arm swing helps walking performance, ask your students to eliminate one of the dependent variables in the experiment—small talk. These 3 walks should be done by each student individually and without socializing. There will be plenty of time for talk in the open discussion portion of Workshop 5.

6 Suggestions

The best way to ensure a no arm swing walk is to have your students hold their workbooks with *both hands,* either in front of or behind them. In the easy arm swing walk, students should move their arms naturally in the plane of motion. In the high-energy arm swing walk, their arms move horizontally back and forth, almost as if pulling on a tug rope that runs through the center of the walker's stomach.

7 Lesson Closure

Consider summarizing the lesson by asking your students if they walked faster with the high-energy arm swing. You might also explain it this way to them: "The faster you move your arms, the faster your legs and feet move, and the faster you can walk. By increasing your arm swing, you are adding power or thrust to your walking motion.

8 Homework

Besides answering a series of TRUE/FALSE questions for homework, students are to *observe* 3 walkers in their neighborhood or at school and *comment* on their arm swing motion.

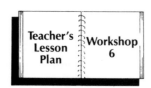

Posture Walk

1 Objectives

A. to teach students the principles of good walking posture
B. to tune-up each student's walking performance by means of posture improvement(s)
C. to practice observation skills

2 The Workshop Plan

After splitting your class into 2-student *teams* (the buddy system), each team will walk *one* lap of the Straw Walk course. For half that lap one buddy will play the role of *walker,* the other will be the *observer.* The observer critiques his or her buddy (walker) based on the *six points of posture.* Halfway through that lap, the buddies switch roles.

In a follow-up lap (Posture Walk 2), the buddies try to improve their posture while under observation again. Finally in Posture Walk 3, the students apply their learning in a maximal effort walk.

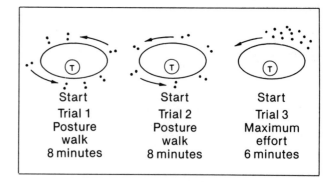

3 Teacher Preparation

As teacher you may want to demonstrate the points of posture to your students so that they know what to look for. You may also want to have one student volunteer join you for a quick demonstration of how to play walker/observer in the buddy system. For the last lap (Posture Walk 3) you will need a *stop watch* to call out finish times.

4 Conducting the Workshop

A. Try to keep the teams fairly isolated to minimize distractions from neighboring buddies. This is a *one-on-one, give and take* workshop. The more 2 buddies can concentrate on each other, the more they will each learn. To accomplish a fair amount of isolation, send each team out at approximately 30 second intervals. As each team starts out on their posture walk, comment to the rest of your students waiting in line to start.

B. Try to allocate your workshop time such that both Posture Walks 1 and 2 are completed in 15 to 20 minutes. Posture Walk 3 (fast) takes less than 4 minutes. That leaves 5 to 10 minutes for open discussion, lesson summary, and a brief explanation of the homework.

5 Potential Pitfalls

Knowing that they are being observed, some of your more self-conscious students may tighten up, which will only distort their natural walking posture. Tell everyone to relax, walk normally, and try to forget that your buddy is out there observing you.

6 Suggestions

Make sure your students are taking notes, not only when they critique but when they are being critiqued. As a guideline, they should limit their commentary at the halfway point of each lap to 1 to 2 minutes.

If time is running short, drop Posture Walk 3. It is more important to summarize this lesson for your students.

7 Lesson Closure

This is a great opportunity to explore what your students have learned about their posture. Ask for volunteers. Have them do quick demonstrations. Do a few yourself if it helps reinforce a point. Ask everyone to identify the *one* point of posture that they need practice the most.

8 Homework

For homework, students will repeat the Posture Walks, but with new partners. Encourage them to enlist an adult for their new walking buddy (partner).

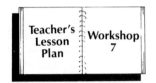

Teacher's Lesson Plan — Workshop 7

Walking Calories

1 Objectives

A. to learn the relationship between *food calories* and *energy expended walking*.
B. to learn to judge the *caloric content* of foods
C. to gain a little "open mouth" consciousness
D. to appreciate certain food types (vegetables and fruit) as opposed to junk foods
E. to improve *team communication skills*
F. to practice mathematics by adding up and multiplying calories and balancing the energy equation

2 The Workshop Plan

Walking Calories is a *team workshop*. All students receive a snack pack containing 5 foods. Each team becomes 1 of the *5* foods that make up the snack pack (the

Apples, Red Team; the Carrots, Orange Team; etc.). The goal of each team is to walk the distance they feel is necessary to burn off their food item. Thus the 6 members of the Apples, after having eaten their 16 calorie slices of apple, need to figure out how far to walk to burn up 16 calories. For the Apples there are two unknowns: (1) the number of calories in the apple slice (¼ section) and (2) the number of calories being burned as they walk.

As the Apples lead the way, you and the rest of your class are to follow them.

When the Apples reach an agreement to stop, you and all your students should stop too. Then ask your class: "Did the Apples walk far enough, or did they walk too far?" Briefly discuss this question, then give the Carrots their turn. After eating the carrot stick, start walking behind the Carrots from the point where the Apples stopped. Continue this procedure until each team has completed their walk.

Summary Procedure in Sequence
A. Each student eats the appropriate food item
B. The appropriate team steps forth and walks
C. When that team stops, there is open discussion
D. Everyone fills in their food charts
E. Teacher announces the correct answer
F. The next food item is eaten as the team representing that food item steps forth to lead the way

To become the walking nutrition expert, study the chart below. It gives you all the answers so that you can settle any arguments that might arise on the Straw Walk course.

Note 1: After each team stops and everyone comments, you should intervene to announce the *correct answer.* At that point everyone should fill in columns (3), (4), and (5) on their *Walking Calories chart.*

Note 2: Walking the distance between any set of $^1/_{10}$ markers on the Straw Walk course (that is, from the $^3/_{10}$ marker to the $^4/_{10}$ marker), burns about 2 calories of food energy. Thus the apple requires walking 8 markers; the carrot, 5 markers; the almond, 3 markers; the celery, 1 marker; and the M & M, 3 markers. It takes 2 full laps (20 markers) to burn off all the food (40 calories) in the snack pack.

Team Color	(1) Walk Description	(2) Food Eaten	(3) Calories Eaten	(4) Calories Burned	(5) Distance Walked (Number of 1/10 Markers)
Red	Apple Walk	¼ Apple	16	16	8
Orange	Carrott Walk	3" Carrot	10	10	5
Yellow	Almond Walk	1 Almond nut	6	6	3
Green	Celery Walk	3" Celery	2	2	1
Blue	M & M Walk	1 M & M	6	6	3
TOTALS.			40 Cal.	40 Cal.	20

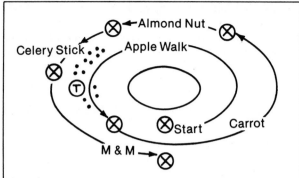

Note: If done correctly, the 5 walks (apple, carrot, almond, celery, and M & M) would total 8 + 5 + 3 + 1 + 3 markers or 20 markers or 2 full laps of the Straw Walk Course.

3 Teacher Preparation

A. This workshop needs to be coordinated with school cafeteria personnel. On the morning of this *Walking Calorie* Workshop, you will need enough snack packs prepared for all of your students. The 5 foods that go into a snack pack can be proportioned out a day ahead of time, loaded into small plastic sandwich bags, and refrigerated (There's nothing like a chilly M & M.). The apple slice may turn a little brown overnight, so you may want to chop the apples into quarters on the day of the workshop.

4 Conducting the Workshop

To save time, assemble your students and your snack packs on the edge of the Straw Walk course. Next split your students into teams and explain the workshop. Do not hand out the snack packs until you are ready to start walking.

5 Potential Pitfalls

A. Give plenty of advance warning to your cafeteria staff so that the *complete* snack pack can be loaded in time for all workshops.

B. To maintain focus on the *"team of the moment,"* keep other teams behind the lead team.

C. Do not hand out snack packs until the last moment before the Apples start the first walk. Otherwise you may not have any snack pack food remaining for the workshop.

D. Be on the alert for food fights. The least appetizing food is usually the first airborne.

6 Suggestions

A. Ask your teams to stop exactly even with a $^1/_{10}$ marker. This will simplify the arithmetic. If that team thinks they need to walk longer, they can walk up to the next $^1/_{10}$ marker. (The distance between $^1/_{10}$ markers is 44 yards.)

B. To save time, the next new team should start walking from where the preceding team stopped.

C. If a student does not feel like eating an item in the snack pack, do not force it. Just let that student pretend as if he or she had eaten the item.

D. Scoring on the *Walking Calories* chart: Always have your students fill in their charts after each walk. For example, if the Apples walk 6 markers, everyone writes a 6 in column (5), and multiplies 6 by 2 and writes 12 in column (4). After you announce that the ¼ apple had 16 calories, everyone can write 16 in column (3).

E. Keep reemphasizing the 2-calorie-per-marker relationship to your class. In other words, everytime you walk 44 yards (the distance between a set of markers) you burn off about 2 calories.

7 Lesson Closure

A. Upon completing your last walk (the M & M Walk), make sure all students have recorded all their data in columns (3), (4), and (5).

B. Have all your students sum up column (3), and then columns (4) and (5). Ask your class to compare column (3) to column (4). How do they compare? Did you walk off more food than you ate? Or did you eat more food calories than you walked off? Ask your class: "What has this workshop taught you about *walking and weight control?*"

8 Homework

The Walking Calories homework is a series of multiple choice questions.

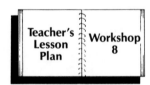

Meal–Walk

1 Objectives

A. to help students understand the importance of a balanced diet

B. to discourage students from eating high-fat meals, typical of those served by the fast-food industry

C. to educate students on the relationship of saturated fats to heart disease

D. to have students communicate in teams to reinforce their knowledge of good eating behavior

E. to show students that *diet* and *exercise* are both important

2 The Workshop Plan

Again students will function in teams, the same teams as in Workshop 7. This time each team will need to choose the best meal to replace the calories burned during their walk. They will be making their decision as they walk 4 laps (1 mile) of the Straw Walk course. After the walk, each team will discuss its decision.

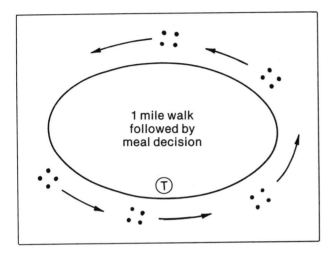

1 mile walk
followed by
meal decision

3 Teacher Preparation

Be prepared to answer student questions in the *postwalk* discussion regarding the *food content* of each of the 8 meal choices. This will require you to become familiar with the *Nutritional Report Card* on page 34.

4 Conducting the Workshop

A. Essentially this is a 2-part workshop involving (1) *team walk/talk* and (2) *class discussion*. Throughout the walk, make sure that teammates stick close together in conversation. Keep teams separated.

B. After 20 minutes all teams should have finished their 4 laps, at which time you should call everyone together for the team discussion.

5 Potential Pitfalls

Time will be the biggest concern in Workshop 8. You want to make sure that enough time remains at the end for group discussion and lesson closure.

6 Suggestions

A. To save time, immediately ask your class to divide up into the same Red, Orange, Yellow, Green, and Blue teams as in Workshop 7.

B. Send the teams off on a staggered basis, minute after minute, and remind them to focus on the foods they think would make a best meal.

C. Remind your children that they need to focus on 2 things in choosing their meal: *total calories* and *the types of calories*.

D. Occasionally tag along at the side of a team to see how the students are doing.

E. Give each team a final lap warning so the students can end their discussion.

7 Lesson Closure

The key points for the lesson summary are:

A. Walking 1 mile, burns approximately 80 calories.

B. Meals 1, 2, 3, 5, 7, and 8 all exceed the 80 calorie limit; in fact, they fall between 150 and 300 calories. Meals 1, 2, 3, 5, 7, and 8 are poor choices for yet another reason—they are all much too high in *fat content*, especially *saturated animal fat*.

C. Meal 4 (½ a plain baked potato) is a good choice as is meal 6 (raw salad combo). Both are *low fat* meals, containing the same number of calories spent in this workshop.

D. So in effect, this workshop has been a lesson in the *quantity* and *quality* of food calories.

E. It would also be worthwhile to discuss the communication process by which teams arrived at their final decisions.

8 Homework

The homework questions reinforce the importance of a balanced diet, with major emphasis on reduction of *saturated fats* for good *cardiovascular health*.

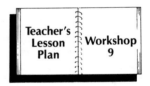

Teacher's Lesson Plan | Workshop 9

Walking Off Weight

1 Objectives

A. to emphasize that *middle-intensity walking* at 3½ to 4 MPH on a regular basis will burn fat and help control weight

B. to reinforce the principles of good teamwork and communication

C. to practice 3½ to 4 MPH aerobic walking with consistant pacing techniques

2 The Workshop Plan

Divide your class into 3 teams. Each team will receive 8 *straws* that represent the 8 *pounds* of excess fat that team needs to lose (hypothetically, of course). The scoring system for losing the excess *pounds* (straws) follows. For each lap of the Straw Walk course walked, that team will be given the following weight reduction credit:

A. *Walk 1 lap* at 3½ to 4 MPH (a 4:17 to 3:45 lap) and your teacher will take 2 straws away from you (2 pound weight loss) plus your team can continue walking.

B. *Walk* 1 *lap* slower than 3½ MPH (slower than a 4:17 lap) and your teacher will take 1 straw away from you (1 pound weight loss) plus your team can continue walking.

C. *Walk* 1 *lap* faster than 4 MPH (faster than a 3:45 lap) and your teacher will take 3 straws away from you (3 pound weight loss), but your team will be benched for 1 *lap* for which your team will be given back 1 straw (1 pound weight gain). Thus each team can complete 4 laps (if they do not get benched). The best possible performance is an 8 straw loss (4 × 2 = 8), achieved by walking a steady 3½ to 4 MPH pace.

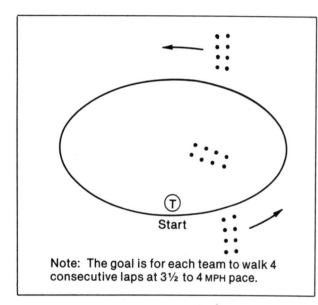

Note: The goal is for each team to walk 4 consecutive laps at 3½ to 4 MPH pace.

3 Teacher Preparation

As teacher, you will need to have the following ready: *a stop watch*, about *40 straws* (8 straws per team plus extras), and a *chart pad* to keep a record of each team's lap time.

4 Conducting the Workshop

The key to this workshop in one word is *timing*. Each team's performance is based on how well they control their speed on the Straw Walk course. To help you man-

age *time*, review the following step-by-step procedure and consider using the chart below to keep tabs on each team's laps.

A. You will need to start each team separately—Red, Orange, and Yellow.

B. To simplify matters, start a team every minute, on the minute.

C. When the first team completes a lap, call out their lap time and mark it on your chart. They should do the same. Take 1, 2, or 3 straws away from their team leader and permit them to continue (as long as they did not exceed 4 MPH).

D. Next, be prepared for the Orange team that will be arriving about 1 minute later.

E. If you bench a team, keep them benched for exactly 4 minutes, such that if they finished their first lap at 3:15, they will start their third lap at 7:15.

To lose 2 straws, a team must finish their lap in the specified time range shown above. If a team takes too much time, they will have to give up only 1 straw! If they are too fast, they get benched.

5 Potential Pitfalls

A. If you fail to start the teams out at the proper time, your scoring system will not be accurate. Remember to start a team *every minute, on the minute*.

B. Each team will be rather large, possibly 8 to 10 in number. It is important for teammates to stick together, walking and talking about their pace.

C. In collecting straws, try not to slow up the team. *One* person, the *team captain*, should hold all the straws for his or her team.

6 Suggestions

A. As shown below, have the teams walk in an orderly formation of 2 rows.

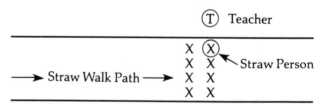

B. Since a 3½ mph lap takes 4:17 and a 4 mph lap takes 3:45, you can average these 2 speeds to sim-

Teacher's Score Card

	Start	Pace	Lap 1	Lap 2	Lap 3	Lap 4 (Finish)
Red Team	0:00	4.0 MPH	3:45	7:30	11:15	15:00
		3.5 MPH	4:17	8:35	12:50	17:10
		—:—	—:—	—:—	—:—	
Orange Team	1:00	4.0 MPH	4:45	8:30	12:15	16:00
		3.5 MPH	5:17	9:35	13:50	18:10
		—:—	—:—	—:—	—:—	
Yellow Team	2:00	4.0 MPH	5:45	9:30	13:15	17:00
		3.5 MPH	6:17	10:35	14:50	19:10
		—:—	—:—	—:—	—:—	

plify the arithmetic by allowing your students a 4:00 ∓ 15 second "time window" per lap.

C. Keep in mind that after Lap 1, each team is being judged on its cumulative time. Thus a team can be going too fast or too slow and still be within the "time window" as long as they average 4-minute laps.

D. Try to anticipate each team's arrival 20 seconds in advance of their reaching the finish line. Use those 20 seconds to figure out whether they are to lose *1*, *2*, or *3* straws.

7   Lesson Closure

Use the last 10 minutes of the workshop to review *total team performance.*

A. Which team lost the most weight?

B. How did everyone feel about the group communication process?

C. What could have been done better?

D. What does this lesson prove to you regarding real-life weight loss?

Answer: Real-life weight loss is best achieved by regular periods of extended, middle-intensity aerobic walking. Half-hour walks at a 3½ to 4 MPH pace can and will do the job!

8   Homework

To help prove this last point and to give students a real-life chance to practice Walking for Weight Control, a special homework project is outlined out on page 38. It is advisable to review this assignment with your students before Workshop 9 adjourns.

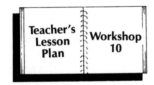

Tobaccoless Road—Part 1

1   Objectives

A. to strengthen children's commitment against all forms of tobacco

B. to give children a chance to influence adults in a positive way

C. to encourage children to think creatively on a walk and practice putting those thoughts on paper in a sincere letter

D. to teach children about the ill-effects of tobacco

E. to let children practice group communication

2   The Workshop Plan

In teams, students will go on a walk down *Tobaccoless Road,* which can be any safe road or path originating from your school grounds. During this walk, team-

mates will need to identify tobacco users who they would like to influence by writing a personal letter to them. Throughout the walk, students should talk about how they plan to write their letters. On returning to school, each team will have a few minutes to elect a team spokesperson who will summarize the team's progress. Then, each spokesperson will address the total class in a brief, 2-minute speech of his or her Tobaccoless Road achievements.

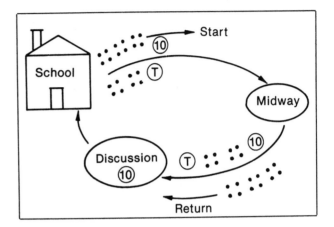

3   Teacher Preparation

For Tobaccoless Road—Part 1, you should review the material on pages 39 through 42. Be prepared to assist those students who are having trouble composing their letters.

4   Conducting the Workshop

A. In Tobaccoless Road you will be walking along with your students. Move from team to team to check their progress. Remember, each student should be identifying his or her own tobacco user.

B. One of the most important parts of this workshop is the group discussion at the end. Make sure you return to school with at least 10 minutes to spare in the class period so each team spokesperson can have a few minutes to summarize his or her team's ideas.

Try to set a specific target date for Workshop 11 (Tobaccoless Road—Part 2) so that students will feel some pressure to write, deliver, and pursue a response to their letters.

5   Potential Pitfalls

A. Should there be a tobacco user on a team, an awkward situation may develop. First the tobacco student may withdraw from conversation, or he or she may try to be disruptive. As teacher you can invite such tobacco students to let this be their chance to reform. You can also suggest to everyone else that they might consider addressing their letters to fellow classmates (or teachers) who they know smoke or chew tobacco.

B. Often all the members of a team will single out *1* tobacco user and address their letters to that *1* person. That is OK if everyone is fairly close to that person and feels a deep commitment to him or her. However, it is *not* OK just for the sake of copying. As you walk along, moving from team to team, encourage everyone to come up with their own best candidate.

6 Suggestions

A. When splitting your class into teams, think about 2 factors: (1) What size team would make a good conversational walking group, and (2) if each team spokesperson took 2 minutes to summarize his or her teammates discussion, how many minutes would be needed at the end of the class to give each spokesperson a chance to speak. (About 5 to 6 students per team yields 5 teams per class, which is reasonable for this workshop.)

B. Try to limit your Tobaccoless Road walks to 20 minutes maximum (10 minutes out, 10 minutes back). This will leave 10 minutes for group discussion at the end of the workshop.

7 Lesson Closure

End this workshop by emphasizing the homework. Students *must* write, deliver, and receive a response to their letters. Students should copy their letters, word for word, in their Student Workbook. Set a definite date for part 2 of Tobaccoless Road.

8 Homework

Read page 42 in the Student Workbook carefully and reinforce the 3 key steps your students will need to take.

A. Write and deliver a letter.
B. Receive a response.
C. Be prepared to discuss that response.

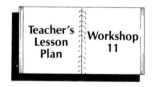

Tobaccoless Road—Part 2

1 Objectives

The objectives of Workshop 11 are the same as Workshop 10.

2 The Workshop Plan

During a short 10-minute walk (same teams from Workshop 10), the students should discuss the responses they received to their letters. After that walk, the teams should regroup at school to record their accomplish-

ments. Each team should then elect a *new* spokesperson to summarize the team's individual accomplishments. *All* students should be taking notes on the responses their classmates received (see page 45).

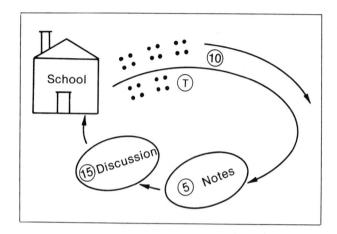

3 Teacher Preparation

Thoroughly read pages 43 through 46 in the Student Workbook.

4 Conducting the Workshop

This is one workshop in which you could use a few hours for the class discussion. Considering you may only have 30 minutes, you must limit the initial walk to 10 minutes and the internal team discussion to about 5 minutes. That will leave 15 minutes for the group discussion.

5 Potential Pitfalls

In the postwalk discussion period some of the more talkative students may take too much time talking about their letters and the responses they received. As teacher, try to circulate among the teams to make sure that *all* students are getting some chance to share their Tobaccoless Road experiences. Similarly in the group discussion period, monitor the situation and put a time limit on any speaker, if necessary.

6 Suggestions

A. If time permits, allow one student to read his or her letter.
B. Ask your class if anyone was really surprised by the response they received from his or her letter.

7 Lesson Closure

Ask your students if they would like to volunteer what they have learned from the Tobaccoless Road Workshops. It might be worth making the point: "Changes do not always occur overnight, but rather gradually over a longer period of time." Ask your class "Who thinks they've made enough progress to want to continue this effort?" Here the word *continue* could mean more persuasion, more letters, following through on a promise, or any of a number of actions that would help the tobacco user finally quit.

8 Homework

One of the most important parts of this homework assignment is the Tobaccoless Road Pledge. Read it out loud to your students and ask for a show of hands for all those who are ready to sign it. That could be a very effective way to end the workshop.

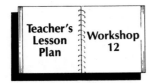

Your Planet Earth

1 Objectives

A. to have children discover and appreciate their environment by walking
B. to give children a chance to practice their journalism skills
C. to sharpen children's ability to observe and record details
D. to have students appreciate how walking can enhance their awareness of everything around them

2 The Workshop Plan

As teacher and guide, take your class on a short walking field trip of approximately 1 mile (closed loop) in the vicinity of your school. Every 5 minutes have your class stop to make detailed observations and to record those observations. After 2 minutes of note taking, resume your walk. After returning to school, give your class a few moments to review their notes. Then ask for volunteers to speak on their observations.

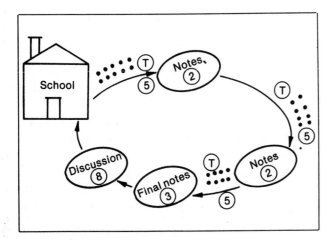

3 Teacher Preparation

Think about some scenic and interesting sites that would make for a good discovery walk. These sites should be located close to your school.

4 Conducting the Workshop

Try allocating about ¾ of this workshop to *walking and writing* (playing news reporter). Save the balance for postwalk discussion and final lesson summary.

5 Potential Pitfalls

Make sure that on this nature walk your students do not get so fascinated by one aspect of the environment that they forget to pay attention to road traffic. Never stop on the shoulder of a road to record notes. In addition, do not walk so far away from school that it takes you the rest of the class period to return. By checking the time and knowing how far you have walked to the site, you should be able to time your return in such a way that you still have 8 or more minutes remaining for the postwalk discussions.

6 Suggestions

Focus on simple things. Tell your students they do not need to find the "eighth wonder" of the world. Remind them to use all of their senses (smell, hearing, sight, taste, and touch) in exploring their environment. Ask them to pay close attention to anything they've never noticed before.

7 Lesson Closure

Ask for volunteers to talk about their observations. How can you as teacher build on these observations to make a concluding statement about "Our Planet Earth" and "How Walking Lets Us Discover It!"

8 Homework

Read page 50 and explain to the students their short-story writing assignment. Students with more complete workshop notes will find these short stories easier to write.

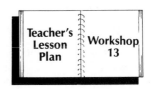

Dealing With Stress

1 Objectives

A. to help students recognize stress within their lives
B. to show students the value of *walking* and *talking* in order to reduce stress

C. to give students practice in helping each other reduce stress

2 The Workshop Plan

After selecting their "worst worries" from a checklist, students will split into mini-teams of 3 to discuss those worries on a relaxing walk. On returning to school, everyone will have a chance to describe their "new" feelings and thoughts.

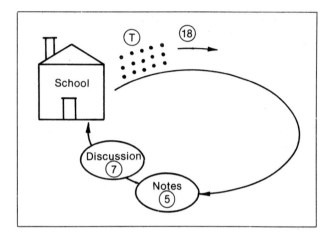

3 Teacher Preparation

To prepare for Workshop 13 read pages 51–54. Think about where you would like your students to take their *stress reduction walk*. Also consider how you will split your class into groups of 3. By random split? By use of the color deck? By alphabetical order?

4 Conducting the Workshop

Allow approximately ⅔ of this workshop (20 minutes) for the *stress reduction walk*. Before starting this walk, have your students take an inventory of stress within their lives by filling out the *All-Time Worry Checklist* on page 52. As the walk progresses, move along with your class, but try to let them function on their own. After returning to school, give your students about 5 minutes to record their feelings about stress and the benefits of walking; then let anyone who would like to share their feelings do so.

5 Potential Pitfalls

It would be much easier for students to communicate with each other on a longer walk. The problem is time—living with the 30-minute class period. In such a short time span, a student may not feel close enough to share a problem with a peer. If anything, the outdoor walking should help students relax. In addition, a student may have a very personal problem that is "off limits" for discussion. Such a student can still play the role of listener, helping to hear and understand a teammate's problem. After a while, such a student may open up by discussing a minor worry, and from there, go on to discuss the bigger concern.

6 Suggestions

In this workshop setting the *right* mood is critical for open communication. One way to accomplish this as a teacher is to turn the workshop over to your students. Would you be willing to switch places with one student who would act as "Teacher of the Day" to lead this workshop?

7 Lesson Closure

As Workshop 13 closes, students should comment on how they can deal with stress in their lives. Draw from these remarks to make a closing statement on the effectiveness of *walking* and *talking* with friends as a way to reduce stress.

8 Homework

This assignment is an extension of Workshop 13—a follow-up walk with a person whom the student feels at ease with. You might ask for volunteers to name the person whom they plan to communicate with on this next stress-reduction walk.

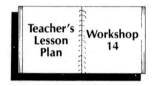

A Walk Across America

1 Objectives

A. to teach students to prioritize based on real needs in a survival situation
B. to reinforce the principles of teamwork and group communications
C. to activate the imagination of children; to start thinking about our country, its geography and terrain, and what it would be like crossing it
D. to improve student understanding of weather and seasonal climate changes
E. to develop a child's sense of independence

2 The Workshop Plan

After dividing your class into 5 teams (Red, Orange, Yellow, Green, and Blue), announce this prime team objective:

> "To select from an 18-item list the 10 *Most Essential Items* you would want to carry with you on *A Walk Across America.*"

Read to your class the ground rules on pages 56 and 57. Be sure to emphasize that this is a 4-month, 3000-mile expedition from the Pacific to the Atlantic, and that each team will have to decide on the *best 10 items* (out of the 18 items listed) during the next *16 minutes* of walking in this workshop. After returning to school the teams should quickly select spokespersons to give 2 minute summaries of their team's *"Big 10"* decisions.

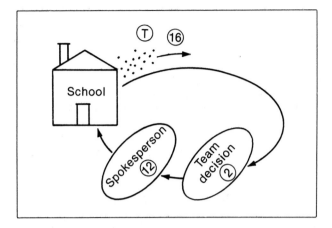

3 Teacher Preparation

Think about where your students should walk on this problem-solving session. Walking down an actual road is a more realistic representation of *Walking Across America.* Walking on the Straw Walk course is safer and more easily controlled. Getting students to use their imaginations is the key, whether it be on a grass field or a strip of asphalt.

4 Conducting the Workshop

Time again is at a premium so students will need to make quick decisions. Team spokespersons will need to summarize their teams' decisions in a 2-minute speech.

5 Potential Pitfalls

Any team may take more time on one particular item. For example, "Should we take the *snake bite kit?"* In addition there may be some internal disagreements about which items to take. This is OK; it is to be expected. What is most important is *how* each team arrives at a final decision.

6 Suggestions

Emphasize the *hint* given on page 57 of the *Student Workbook*—the point that it may be easier to arrive at a decision by *ruling out 8* items, rather than *trying to pick 10.* Encourage your students to take quick notes throughout their walk. Each team should elect a secretary-recorder just for this purpose. By the end of the walk, all teammates should have recorded their team's final 10 items. *What are the 10 best items?* Actually there is *no one best solution!* What one person or team feels is important may not be considered essential by the next. If you elected to take the *snake bite kit,* but never saw a snake, were you wrong? What if you didn't take the *snake bite kit,* but you worried yourself into an ulcer thinking about rattlesnakes along the road? Should you have taken the snake bite kit just for peace of mind? And so on.

As far as the real face value of each item, you might want to be aware of the following:

1. *SNOWSHOES* Probably will not be needed because Highway Departments clear the roads immediately after storms. They are not easy to walk in; besides, walking from September through December (reaching New York in December) you wouldn't expect a major snow accumulation.

2. *FLASHLIGHT* Good to have on the road at night, but one might question whether it's even safe to be out on the highway in the dark. The support vehicle has full lighting too.

3. *ROAD MAPS* Certainly important, but couldn't they be bought along the way, state by state?

4. *SNAKE BITE KIT* The chances of getting bitten by a poisonous snake while walking on a road in daylight is near *zero* probability.

5. *WARM MITTENS* Crossing the Rocky Mountains at high altitude you will find temperatures dropping 5°f for every 1,000 feet of elevation. Winter in Appalachia Mountain will be cold too at the end of the journey in December.

6. *FOOT CARE KIT* It is difficult to appreciate the importance of good foot care until you have walked across America, or until you have experienced your first blister on a big walk. Your basic Blister Prevention and Treatment Kit consists of foot powders, moisturizing creams, bandages, disinfectants, and a sterile needle to puncture and drain swollen blisters.

7. *RADIO HEADSET* This is probably one of the worst contraptions to take on the road because it eliminates one of your greatest assets—hearing. Listening to road traffic is essential for survival. Forget the radio!

8. *CANTEEN AND WATER* One needs to look at the potential for dehydration, especially in the desert. Actually for a fall to winter walk, the desert is the only main stretch where water should be a concern. However, couldn't a lightweight 16-ounce plastic bottle of club soda accomplish the same?

9. *CAMERA AND FILM* How important is photographic documentation to you? This is a personal decision that needs to be weighed against other basic survival items.

10. *$1,500 IN TRAVELERS CHECKS* It's always good to carry money when you travel—for food, supplies, and unseen emergencies. Travelers checks are safe; $1,500 allows you about $12 per day, which should be fine considering that your support vehicle is a *free* motel room each night.

11. *$1,000 IN CASH* Would you want to be carrying this much cash with you when you cross America? Besides, if you took $1,500 in Travelers Checks, would you need another $1,000 in cash?

12. *TOOTHBRUSH AND DENTAL FLOSS* Walking across America is no excuse for poor hygiene. Daily brushing and flossing of the teeth is essential.

13. *SHOES AND SOCKS* Once again, the comfort of the feet are so critical. How could you not give your right and left feet the best walking equipment available?

14. *RAINPROOF JACKET AND PANTS* In all probability it will rain about 20 percent of the days based on the average weather recorded over the last 50 years. By getting wet in a chilly rain, you are susceptible to colds, sore throats, fever, virus, flu, and even hypothermia (rapid loss of body heat potentially leading to death). Strongly consider an all-weather, breathable, waterproof top and bottom suit.

15. *TOP/BOTTOM WOOL LONG JOHNS* Once again, the concern over weather arises. In any cold, damp weather the body requires insulation. Wool is a great insulator. It traps warm air and moisture and keeps the skin from losing heat fast. Used under waterproof garments, such long johns should insulate the body under most severe conditions.

16. *WAIST PACK* Sometimes, called a fanny pack or day pack, this bag straps around the waist directly above the hips. It serves one hundred purposes as a pouch capable of carrying anything from food and water to a foot care kit and maps. The cross-country journeyman doesn't leave home without it.

17. *WALKING JOURNAL AND PEN* Again one needs to weigh the importance of record keeping. When the journey is over, and years from now when your memory is thin and fading thinner, your Walking Journal may be the only thing you have to show for your walk.

18. *INSULATED WATERPROOF HAT AND HOOD* In very cold, damp weather over 60 percent of our heat escapes from our head. It is by far the most important part of our body to protect from the freezing elements. Knowing the lightning speed at which storms and Artic air masses can move into a region of the West, it's near suicide to try to walk without this kind of head protection.

Note: In explaining this assignment to your students, insist that they must pick *10 and only 10* items on the list.

---

7   Lesson Closure

After each spokesperson gives a summary talk of his or her team's strategy, consider asking your students any of these questions:

A. After hearing your teammates, how many of you would change your top 10 choices?
B. How many of you think that you could make it across America on foot in 4 months?
C. What does this Walk Across America Workshop prove to you?

In answer to the last question, consider these points:

A. In life we need to prioritize, and sometimes the decisions are not all that easy.
B. What's important to one person may not be that critical to another.
C. Depending on how we look at it, a problem can have several different correct answers. In other words, life is not all black and white; often there's a lot of gray.

8   Homework

This assignment gives students a chance to use their creative road-mapping skills in plotting their own 50-state walk of America.

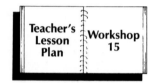

Self-Improvement

1   Objectives

A. to reinforce the principles of aerobic walking, pacing, and cardiovascular conditioning

2   The Workshop Plan

Workshop 15 is divided into 4 exercises:

A. Exercise 1: A 3½ MPH walk similar to Workshop 4
B. Exercise 2: A 4 MPH walk similar to Workshop 4
C. Exercise 3: A trial and error aerobic walk similar to Workshop 2
D. Exercise 4: A final Straw Walk (Workshop 3)

After each walk, students answer questions pertaining to the principles of that exercise.

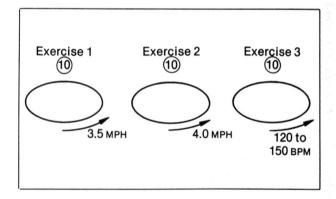

3   Teacher Preparation

A. Review each of the exercises in Workshop 15 in detail by referring back to Workshops 2, 3, and 4 in your Teacher's Curriculum Guide. (*Note:* In this current workshop the exercises are *not* done in teams.)

B. Be prepared to explain the answers to questions 1 through 8 for these 4 exercises.

4 Conducting the Workshop

Spend about 15-20 minutes on each of the 4 exercises in Workshop 15. About half of that time should be devoted to physical walking and the other half to answering the specific questions. You will probably need TWO full periods to complete all 4 exercises.

5 Potential Pitfalls

In each exercise your students will be finishing their laps in a staggered fashion. Therefore, from the time when the first students start coming across the finish line to when the last ones finish their laps, you will need to be ready with your stop watch—calling out lap times and helping students with their 6-second pulse checks. The easiest way to accomplish these pulse checks is to group clusters of students finishing their laps in near proximity so they can all listen simultaneously to your 6-second count.

6 Suggestions

Encourage students to work on their own in each of these exercises. This includes judging their own walking speed (not copying a classmate's pace). It also means answering each question by themselves. After each exercise, review the questions in open discussion.

7 Lesson Closure

This is a great opportunity to make a summary statement on the key principles taught in *Walking Wellness:*

A. Exercise does not need to be painful to be beneficial.

B. Walking is truly aerobic, and as an aerobic exercise it helps condition the heart muscle.

C. Any form of walking—slow, medium, or fast—does the body good.

D. In general, *faster* walking is more beneficial to the *heart*, while *easy* walking over longer stretches is ideal for *weight control.*

E. A good middle intensity aerobic walk will typically raise a child's heart rate to 120–150 BPM.

F. For every minute of walking you do, your body burns about 5 calories of food (compared to 1 calorie of food while sitting).

G. Besides controlling weight, walking is an excellent way to relieve stress.

H. Best of all, walking is so natural and simple, it frees our minds to think creatively.

8 Homework

This assignment reinforces many of the key principles previously studied in workshops 2, 3 and 4 of Walking Wellness.

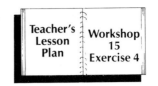

The "Last" Straw Walk

1 Objectives

A. to remeasure each student's aerobic capacity in a 15-minute maximal effort walk (the Straw Walk)

B. to have students measure their Fitness Walking progress by comparing their Straw Walk performances (workshop 3 versus workshop 15)

C. to have students understand the reasons for changes in their walking performance

D. to demonstrate to students that a regular and sensible walking program makes for lifelong fitness.

2 The Workshop Plan

Exercise 4 follows the same basic format as Workshop 3 (The Straw Walk).

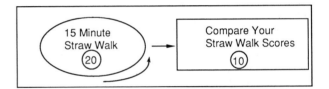

3 Teacher Preparation

Prepare for another Straw Walk. Try to duplicate the "test" conditions such that each child's Straw Walk Score will be on an equivalent basis to previous performances.

4 Conducting the Workshop

Reference: Workshop 3 *Note:* Remember to reserve about 10 minutes at the end of Workshop 15 for reviewing the questions.

5 Potential Pitfalls

Reference: Workshop 3

6 Suggestions

Reference: Workshop 3

7 Lesson Closure

An interesting way to close this workshop is to ask for a show of hands of all those students who improved their Straw Walk scores. Next you might ask "How many of you feel as if you have become more fit?" (show of hands), and "How many of you think you still have room for more improvement?" The last question is your perfect lead into Workshop 16 during which students will begin to formulate their NEW WALKING PROGRAMS.

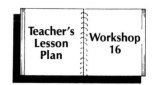

Teacher's Lesson Plan | Workshop 16

Your New Walking Program

1 Objectives

A. to help students establish specific Walking Action Plans aimed at lifelong Wellness

B. to let students share their ideas with their classmates, and in so doing, revise their own plans to their best liking

C. to improve oral communication skills

D. to give students experience in writing a personal action plan.

2 The Workshop Plan

Students split into 5 teams (Red, Orange, Yellow, Green, and Blue) are to take turns discussing their Walking Action Plans with their teammates on a mile walk of the Straw Walk course. After this walk, 5 team spokespersons will be selected to give 2-minute summary speeches of their team's Walking Action Plans. All classmates are to take notes during these speeches to fine-tune their own Walking Action Plans as part of their homework.

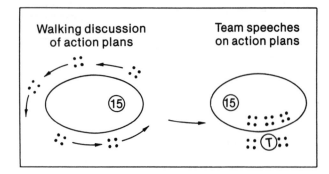

Walking discussion of action plans | Team speeches on action plans

3 Teacher Preparation

Completely reread Workshop 16 both in your Teacher's Curriculum Guidebook and in the Student Workbook.

Also review page 73 (Creative Walking Ideas) in the Appendix.

4 Conducting the Workshop

A. This final workshop is again a 50/50 split (50 percent team walking, 50 percent team discussion). It is important to proportion time this way in order to (1) give each team a fair chance for discussion and (2) let everyone benefit from the variety of ideas of individuals as presented by each spokesperson.

B. Set aside the last 5 minutes of this workshop to explain the homework.

5 Potential Pitfalls

The most difficult part of this workshop is getting all the *voices* and *plans* of your students heard during the team walk when classmates exchange ideas and during the final speeches by each team spokesperson. Anything you as teacher can do to encourage your students to draw the best ideas out of everyone will make Workshop 16 a better success. Each student needs some recognition at this point in the course.

6 Suggestions

Below are some suggestions you can offer to your students: (1) Make it a team goal that everyone gets a chance to discuss their Walking Action Plan on the team walk. (2) Each team could appoint a coordinator—someone who could politely give signals every ½ lap to introduce the next teammate. This way as many as 8 teammates could discuss their Action Plans in 4 laps of walking. (3) Each spokesperson should try to incorporate *at least* one idea from each of his or her teammates in the final summary speech. (4) Every student should be taking notes while each team spokesperson talks.

7 Lesson Closure & Homework

Try to get your students to focus on at least 1 lifestyle change that will make a difference. Sometimes we get overwhelmed by the magnitude to the *task* that faces us—like looking up the wall of Mt. Everest. How will we ever get to the top? Yet if we can just take it a step at a time—as on an 11,208 mile walk—then we can reach our goal. In achieving lifelong wellness, it works the same way. It's the little things we do throughout our lives that will determine our health 5, 10, 20, and 50 years from now. So start small and build up. A simple Walking Action Plan outlining *one* walking lifestyle behavior change is a great start. That is the Workshop 16 homework. It may be the end of the course, but it's just the beginning of a *Walk Down Wellness Road*.

The Homework Answers

Homework in a Physical Education Course?

Walking Wellness comes with homework. In fact, every workshop is followed by an assignment. Your students should complete those assignments *before* their next upcoming workshop. This homework serves 5 prime purposes:

1. it reinforces previous workshops
2. it gives students an opportunity to involve their family members
3. it teaches students to think creatively on walks
4. it reinforces basic education skills
5. it prepares students for their next workshop

The homework assignments take many different forms. There are: (1) *true/false* and *multiple choice* questions, (2) questions based on the *workshop data*, (3) *essay-type* questions and *compositions* to write, (4) *lifestyle planning* projects involving journal keeping and behavioral inventories, and in many cases (5) *family-oriented* homework projects.

To help you review this homework with your students, *Homework Answers* are tabulated on the following pages.

Regarding *grading* and *reviewing* of homework, these are your choices. You can periodically call on students in class to check homework comprehension, or you may occasionally collect student notebooks for homework grading. Sometimes a quiz might be appropriate.

In those Walking Wellness Workshops where time does not permit past homework review, consider devoting a portion of a separate period to a discussion of that particular assignment. Teachers in other subject areas might also want to review those special assignments that reinforce their own curriculums. For example, consider (1) the writing and reading assignments, (2) the assignments involving mathematical computations, (3) the health education homework (stress and tobacco), and (4) the Walk Across America geography assignment.

In summary, it will become obvious from the responses and performances of your students as to *who is* and *who is not* doing their homework. This is one important basis for arriving at *student grades* at the end of the semester.

Homework — Workshop 5

Part (A) Compare your *lap times* in Walks 1, 2 and 3. Did you walk faster when you swung your arms at your sides? _____ YES _____ NO. Why do you think swinging your arms helps you walk better?

_____

_____

Part (B) This week in your neighborhood or at your school, take time out to observe 3 people who are walking. From a fair distance watch how they swing their arms. On the chart below describe their *arm swing* and *how they might improve*.

	Describe Arm Swing	Room For Improvement
Walker 1	_____	_____
Walker 2	_____	_____
Walker 3	_____	_____

Part (C) Answer TRUE or FALSE for each of the statements below by checking the appropriate space.

(1) _____ TRUE _____ FALSE Proper arm swing adds *rhythm* and *timing*, *balance* and *power* to the walking stride.

(2) _____ TRUE _____ FALSE As your left arm swings forward while walking, your left foot moves forward, too.

(3) _____ TRUE _____ FALSE If it took you 800 *right footsteps* and 800 *left footsteps* to walk 1 mile, then your *right and left* arms probably swung forward about 800 times each during that mile walk.

(4) _____ TRUE _____ FALSE Assume your *Straw Walk* score was 3.7 without hardly any arm-swing action in your walk. If you increased your arm-swing energy, you would expect your *Straw Walk* score to increase.

(5) _____ TRUE _____ FALSE As you swing your arms faster and harder on a walk, it is likely that your walking heart rate will decrease.

Part (D) Read pages 23–26 to prepare for Workshop 6.

22 ★ ★ ★ End of Workshop 5 ★ ★ ★

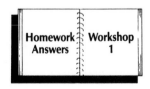

Homework Answers — Workshop 1

A Walking Field Trip

PARTS (A) (B) (C) (Page 4) The object is to try to get children to think about all those places that they really could walk to instead of depending on Mom and Dad and the family "cab."

PART (D) Your student's response to this question may give you some creative ideas for future *Walking Field Trips.* Consider for example:

A WALK TO THE:	TO LEARN ABOUT:
Bakery	Baking Techniques
Post Office	U.S. Mail System
Museum or Famous Landmark	Local History
Farm/Ranch	Agriculture/Livestock
Forest/River	Nature/Conservation
Police/Fire Station	Security/Safety
Construction Site	Engineering
Public Health Organization	Disease Prevention
Social Service Organization	Volunteerism
Hospital	Health Care
Senior Citizen Center	Elderly Activities
Mechanics Shop	Engine Design
Local Newspaper	Journalism
Stock Broker	The Stock Market
Real Estate Broker	Land Investment

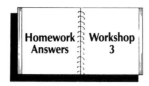

Homework Answers / Workshop 2

Aerobic Walking

PARTS (A) (B) (Page 8) For the average child, you would expect the following heart rate responses:

Lying still in bed	50 – 60 BPM
After brushing teeth	60 – 90 BPM
After climbing stairs	140 – 180 BPM
After brisk walking	120 – 150 BPM

PART (C) Only *stair climbing* and *brisk walking* would qualify as aerobic exercise, the safest being *brisk walking.* When you exercise aerobically, the following physical feelings occur:

1. possible onset of sweat
2. slight body temperature rise (warm feeling)
3. heavier breathing (but not too uncomfortable)
4. consistent, rhythmic body movement without sudden fatigue

Homework Answers / Workshop 3

The Straw Walk

QUESTION (1) Most students will probably walk further (and thus score higher) in their second Straw Walk mainly because of improved pacing technique. Some will do better simply by trying harder. Others may im-

prove their scores as a result of improved cardiovascular conditioning from their fitness walking program.

QUESTION (2) This question is intended to help children set new fitness goals for themselves. Based on test scores nationwide, it is not unreasonable to expect an average child to improve his or her Straw Walk Score by as much as ONE STRAW (1 mph) over the course of the school year.

QUESTION (3) A child's Straw Walk performance is related to a number of performance factors as outlined on page 12 in the Student Workbook. Question (3) asks children to re-examine those performance factors to determine which ones are most influential in their own lives. For example, Johnny may realize that his overweight condition is preventing him from reaching high walking speeds. However, if he set a goal to cut out some high-fat junk foods, and drop a few pounds in weight, then maybe he could bring his Straw Walk Score up from a 3.5 to a 4.0.

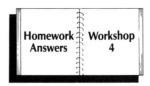

Homework Answers / Workshop 4

Teamwalks

PART (A) QUESTIONS (1) through (4):

Here we are looking to see if the student is aware of the importance of TEAMWORK and how it might be improved.

PART (B) QUESTIONS (5) & (6):
ANSWERS: (5)E, (6)E

PART (C) The major differences between 3½ and 4 mph walking are that at 4 mph you work harder, sweat more, breathe faster, fatigue faster, tighten up quicker in the legs and burn calories quicker.

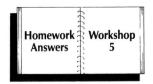

Walking in Rhythm

PART (A) (Page 22) By swinging your arms you add balance to your body. With that comes body rhythm to help the timing of each footstep. The arm swing adds power too, helping you to increase your stride and overall thrust.

PART (C) (1) TRUE (2) FALSE (3) TRUE (4) TRUE (5) FALSE

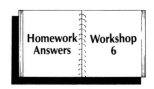

Posture Walk

PART (A) (Page 26) Student answers will vary considerably depending on the specific walkers involved.

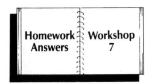

Walking Calories

PART (A) (Page 30) (1) E Remember, 2 calories for every set of markers walked. (2) B (3) B 4 laps = 40 markers × 2 = 80 calories. (4) E 1 lap is worth about 20 calories, 20 laps = 400 calories. (5) C Dividing 40 calories by 5 calories per minute = 8 minutes.

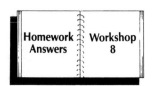

Meal-Walk

PART (A) (page 34) (1) E (2) D (3) E (4) E (5) All fried food, fatty meat, shell fish, excessive candy and cakes, bacon.

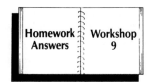

Walking Off Weight

PART (A) (Page 38) *Example:* Suppose that a child set a goal of walking 2 hours per week instead of watching 2 hours of *TV* per week. By walking, a child burns about 300 calories per hour, compared to 60 calories at the TV. The difference here is 600 − 120 or 480 calories per week. On a yearly basis (multiply 480 × 52), that is 25,000 calories. Since a pound of fat contains 3,500 calories, the extra 25,000 calorie difference amounts to a 7 pound weight loss.

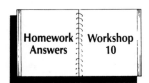

Tobaccoless Road—Part 1

PARTS (A) (B) (C) (Page 42) The student's response to this assignment depends on the individual situation at hand.

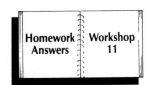

Tobaccoless Road—Part 2

PART (A) (Page 46) (1) TRUE (2) TRUE (3) FALSE (4) TRUE (5) TRUE

PART (B) Actually, there are dozens of reasons a student can cite here: (1) tobacco causes lung cancer; (2) tobacco causes heart disease; (3) tobacco destroys the lung tissue; (4) nicotine destroys blood vessel walls, causing hardening of the arteries; (5) the carbon monoxide in tobacco smoke poisons the blood, causing shortness of breath; (6) smokers have less aerobic endurance and energy; (7) smokers tire faster; (8) smokers often develop deep coughs and sinus colds that seem to go on forever; (9) smokers loose their natural voice and wind up with a deep raspy voice; (10) tobacco users are constantly fighting the problems of bad breath, yellow stained teeth, and stinky clothing; (11) smokers are becoming "social skunks" in environments where people are demanding a circle of clean free air; (12) tobacco users are wasting a fortune of money, not only in buying their tobacco, but in health care costs "down the road"; (13) tobacco users are actually polluting our environment as well as their bodies; (14) tobacco users are setting terrible health examples for the children of tomorrow.

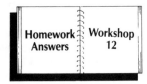

Your Planet Earth

PART (A) (Page 50) The Short Story: Obviously there is no standard answer for this homework assignment. However, if some of your students are searching for ideas and guidance here, it might not be a bad idea to work in cooperation with a few interested English teachers on this assignment.

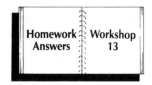

Dealing With Stress

PART (A) (Page 54) Student answers will be specific to the stress-reduction encounter faced.

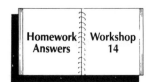

A Walk Across America

PART (A) (Page 58) There are an infinite number of ways to plot a walking path which touches ALL 50 states of America. As you review your student's solutions, ask them: (1) if they considered the weather as a factor, (2) if they could touch 3 or 4 states at one time, (3) which would be their favorite state to visit, and (4) which states would be the hottest, coldest, and wettest.

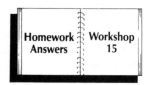

Self-Improvement

WALKING EXERCISE 1 (Page 60) (1) Hopefully most students will have paced themselves at about 3.5 MPH, which translates to a ¼ mile lap time of 4:17 (*Note:* any lap time between 4:10 and 4:25 is reasonably good). (2) B (3) D (4) D

WALKING EXERCISE 2 (Page 60) (5) Again, any lap time between 3:40 and 3:50 is reasonably good. A 3:45 lap time is a perfect 4.0 MPH pace. (6) D

WALKING EXERCISE 3 (Pages 61) (8) For most students aerobic walking will be most beneficial and enjoyable in the middle intensity, aerobic target zone of 120 to 150 heart beats per minute. This is not to say that *higher* or *lower* intensity walking is a poor choice. However in this exercise, we want to make sure that students know how to walk at the *middle intensity level.*

HOMEWORK QUESTIONS (Page 62) (1) and (2) Students should refer back to page 12 to review the specific factors that may have helped or hindered their Straw Walk performance. (3) A (4) C (5) FALSE. Health needs to be a lifelong commitment. It only takes a few weeks to start getting out of shape once you stop exercising. Hence, it's best to select *exercises* that give you *pleasure* and *enjoyment*. These are the kind of activities you will want to keep up for life.

(6) FALSE Exercise is only part of the total Wellness picture, and it CANNOT make up for the damages that occur in the LUNGS and BLOOD VESSELS as a result of SMOKING and POOR DIET. (7) TRUE Absolutely! Tobacco contains nicotine, which is an addictive drug. Once you start using it, the habit becomes more and more difficult to break. So the best way to avoid this addiction is to never start in the first place. However, if a student has made a poor health choice in using tobacco, he or she can still break the habit. It just takes a bit of willpower and a substitution plan. For *example:* Substitute *walking* for *smoking.* (8) FALSE While heredity is a factor in heart disease, *lifestyle health habits* such as *weight and blood pressure control, diet* and *exercise*, and *avoidance of tobacco* have a major impact on a child's chance of either having or surviving a heart attack. (9) FALSE Life is more than a *win-lose game. Health* is so much more important than keeping score of who beat who. In the "game" of health, everyone can be a winner.

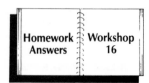

Your New Walking Plan

PARTS (A) (B) (Page 66) Answers dependent on specific creativity of each student.

Post Graduate Walking Wellness

The Post Graduate Walking Wellness Program

If you are wondering how you will continue to develop your students' healthy walking habits after they've completed the **Walking Wellness** curriculum, you may be pleased to know that a post-graduate **Walking Wellness** program does exist. It is based on the workshop principles covered in the original **Walking Wellness** course. The difference is that the post-graduate workshops are designed with new twists to challenge students and reinforce their previous learnings. As you read through this post-graduate section, think about all the creative variations that you could design into these **Walking Wellness** workshops to help keep your children on a positive learning curve.

Post Graduate Workshop #1 A Walking Field Trip

A Workshop Objectives

The primary goal in taking Walking Field Trips is to show children that they are capable of going places on foot without the family taxi. In workshop #1, your students were given the opportunity to visit a nearby "site" on foot.

B New Suggestions

- Let your students work in teams to plan their next walking field trip.
- Encourage your students to increase the length of their walking field trips (for improved endurance).
- Consider using a double period for a 3-mile hike. Perhaps you could combine lunch and a teaching period to take your kids on longer walks.
- Integrate your next walking field trip with lessons in geography, environmental science, urban planning and traffic safety.
- Invite parents and your principal on several follow-up walking field trips.

C Homework

- Have students write a short composition describing places they now walk to (instead of riding) as a result of their Walking Wellness program.
- Set up an awards system in which students receive extra credit for walking to places that they previously would have been driven to.

Post Graduate Workshop #2 Aerobic Walking

A Workshop Objectives

The primary goal of this workshop is to let each child discover for himself the particular walking pace which is ideal for aerobic training (120 to 150 heartbeats per minute).

In workshop #2 each student was asked to walk ¼ mile at a sufficient pace to raise his heart rate up to 120 to 150 beats per minute (the aerobic target zone for most children). At the end of this ¼-mile walk, each child measured his pulse to check how close he came to walking at a heart rate of 120-150 beats per minute. Depending on that performance, children would then either speed up or slow down on their next lap to fine tune their aerobic walking pace.

B New Suggestions

- Inasmuch as a child's cardiorespiratory system will change significantly over the course of a year, it is highly recommended that this exercise be repeated in its entirety using this same "trial and error" procedure (see Workshop #2 in the Student Workbook).
- After your students find their *new* aerobic walking pace, compare this *new* pace to their previous pace.
  NOTE: A year later, most children will find that they will need to walk faster to maintain the same heart rate intensity level (120-150 beats per minute). This can be the result of: (1) cardiovascular conditioning, and (2) general development of the heart muscle, lungs and working muscles.

- Graphing your heart rate response. Take your children on 3 or 4 separate 1-mile walks—each at a distinctly different pace. For example, a *3 mph walk* (20 minutes per mile), a *3-1/2 mph walk* (17 minutes per mile), a *4 mph walk* (15 minutes per mile), etc. Immediately following each walk, have your students measure their heart rates. Then ask each student to record his own heart rate on a graph as shown below:

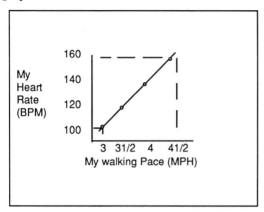

*Note: the heart rate responses shown on this graph may not be typical of what ALL your children would experience.

By completing this project, students should get a very clear understanding of how their hearts respond to an exercise workload.

Post Graduate Workshop #3
The Straw Walk

A Workshop Objectives

Straw Walks accomplish many things. They establish a fitness baseline from which to measure improvement. They teach children how to pace. They transform "plain walking" into a physically challenging event. And most importantly, Straw Walks give children an outstanding 15-minute aerobic workout.

For all these reasons, your students will *always* benefit by doing repeated Straw Walks. Some teachers do 10 to 20 Straw Walks a year! There is **no** better 15-minute aerobic exercise that will safely meet the conditioning needs of **all** your children.

In the original Straw Walk, your students walked around a 1/4-mile Straw Walk course at the fastest pace they could maintain for 15 minutes. Every time they completed a lap, they earned a straw. After 15 minutes, your whistle froze them in place. The number of straws in the student's hand added to the fraction of the last completed lap, gave each child his Straw Walk Score. For example, 4 straws at the 5th cone is a 4.5 mph Straw Walk score—which is equivalent to walking 4.5 mph.

B New Suggestions

- Do not hesitate to start off the new year by having your children participate in a new 15-minute Straw Walk. In doing so, you could have your class compare their **new** Straw Walk scores to their best performance of last year.
- Continue to have your students set new Straw Walk goals for the year. *Training* and *lifestyle* will be the key factors affecting self-improvement.
- To help your students build their confidence levels, you can let them participate in The Little Straw Walk—a 6-minute (1/10th hour) Straw Walk on a 1/10-mile loop. Hence the Straw Walk scores still translate to a mph pace. However, in the Little Straw Walk, students should be able to walk a faster pace since they need to hold that pace for only *6 minutes* (as opposed to 15 minutes).
NOTE: Little Straw Walks are also ideal for K-3 children. The complete Little Straw Walk Workshop is described in Chapter 7 of the book, **Walking for Little Children**.
- Double Straw Walks: If you really want to test the endurance of your students, have them participate in a 30-minute Double Straw Walk in which you hand each child a half straw each time they complete a lap on the 1/4-mile Straw Walk loop. Thus, at the end of 30 minutes, their straws will reflect their mph walking speed—except they have been challenged to go at that pace for twice as long!
NOTE: Any student who can score as well in the Double Straw Walk (compared to the regular Straw Walk) is probably aerobically fit and geared for higher endurance events.

Parent Participation: Consider inviting parents to an open house field day at school to participate in a parent-child Straw Walk. The benefits of conducting this event are:
- Parents will appreciate that walking is good exercise for their children.
- Children will begin to see their parents as role models.
- Straw Walks will inspire some families to start a fitness walking program together.

Your New Teaching Ideas

_____

_____

_____

_____

_____

_____

_____

_____

Post Graduate Workshop #4
Teamwalks

A Workshop Objectives

Teamwalks let children discover what it is like to walk 3-1/2 and 4 mph. Teamwalks also let children practice their listening and communication skills.

B New Suggestions

At the start of the school year, ask a few students at random to demonstrate 3-1/2 and 4 mph pacing. Does it look as if these students still have their walking speedometers calibrated, or do they need a tune up? You might ask the rest of your class this question. Chances are that a number of your students will have lost some of their sensitivity for 3-1/2 and 4 mph pacing. If so, you could divide the class into teams and challenge them to a game of Teamwalk, at 3-1/2 mph or 4 mph.

☐ New Suggestion

Another variation of the Teamwalk is to divide your class into teams of 5 to 6 children. Then have each team walk at their own pace around the Straw Walk loop. As they complete their laps, each team captain guesses (aloud) his team's lap time for that loop. As teacher, you would record each team's guess with their actual time. After everyone reassembles, review each team's performance. How many teams thought they actually walked faster than they really did?

Post Graduate Workshops #5 & #6
Walking in Rhythm and Posture Walk

A Workshop Objectives

Both of these workshops are designed to help children improve their walking posture.

B New Suggestions

- An exciting follow-up to these workshops could be provided by video filming the walking postures of your children. By viewing these walking videos, your students would:
  1. gain greater acceptance of themselves ("Oh! I have a pretty nice gait.")
  2. learn how to "tune up" their walking techniques and posture
  3. become excited about teaching their parents and friends all about walking technique.

☐ New Suggestions

Encourage students to practice good walking posture through such walking games as: *Tunnel Walks, Bean Bag Walks, Puddle Walks, Shadow Walks* and *Line Walks* (see Chapter 8 of **Walking for Little Children**). While each of these games was originally designed for K-3 children, even adults enjoy them and learn when playing them.

Post Graduate Workshop #7
Walking Calories

A Workshop Objectives

In the original Walking Calories workshop, your children split into five teams: *The Apples, The Carrots, The Almond Nuts, The Celery Sticks* and *The M&Ms.* Each team was given the task of walking off the number of calories contained in their food item. For example, kids learn that they need to walk the length of a football field to burn off an M&M.

B New Suggestions

You can present a similar Walking Calories workshop simply by substituting new food items in your snack pack. For example, consider making up new snack packs with some of the foods shown below:

Food Item	Calories	Distance
1 grape	6	3 cones
1 graham cracker	28	14 cones
1/8 orange	10	5 cones
cucumber slice	8	4 cones
1 oatmeal cookie	40	20 cones
1 cashew nut	10	5 cones

The oatmeal cookie, like the M&M, is the big calorie counter. To burn it off, you'd have to walk *2 laps* of the Straw Walk Course. That's 20 cones or 1/2 mile!

Your New Teaching Ideas

_____

_____

_____

_____

_____

_____

_____

C Food Logging Homework

Often it's hard to imagine how much food we really consume in a day. Sometimes it's as if we eat without thinking as the calories add up so quickly. However, if you forced yourself to record everything you ate in a day, you would soon gain an appreciation of your eating behavior. If more people kept food logs—even if for only a few days a month—they wouldn't keep repeating that famous line: "But I've hardly eaten anything today."

As a follow-up project to Walking Calories, have your students maintain a food log of everything they eat (complete description and portions) for several days. In a follow-up discussion, review the food logs of your students. For extra credit, have them calculate their caloric intake on a daily basis and their calorie expenditure as a result of walking. While this assignment does take time, it is a great way for children to learn about weight management.

Post-Graduate Workshop #8
Meal-Walk

A Workshop Objectives

The prime goal of the Meal-Walk workshop is to give children an opportunity to think about and discuss good nutrition while walking in the fresh outdoors. In other words, healthy exercise inspires healthy eating.

During this workshop, children walk in teams for about a mile, discussing 8 meal choices on a given menu, while trying to decide which of those 8 meals is the healthiest.

B New Suggestions

Take your students on a walking field trip to a local grocery store. On the walk and during your visit, think about the following questions:

(1) How many calories are we burning on this field trip?
(2) What foods would replenish these calories?
(3) What are the healthiest and unhealthiest foods in the grocery?
(4) How much would it cost to buy the right foods to prepare a fresh salad?
(5) What are some of the unhealthy foods served in our school cafeteria?
(6) How could we start a project to improve the menu in our school cafeteria?

Post Graduate Workshop #9
Walking off Weight

A Workshop Objectives

The Walking Off Weight workshop teaches students that walking for extended periods of time at a moderate 3.5 to 4 mph pace is the best way to burn fat and lose weight (as opposed to walking very fast for short time intervals).

To emphasize this point, students are split into teams and given 8 new pounds of body fat (8 straws). Each team is told that they can lose their 8 pounds of body fat if they walk around the Straw Walk Course (the teacher collects a certain number of their straws depending on which pace they maintain) at a pace of 3.5 to 4 mph (1 lap every 4 minutes). If they walk faster than 4 mph or slower than 3.5 mph, they will not make their target weight loss goal.

B New Suggestions

Play this same game, except give each walker on the team 8 straws (or 8 new pounds of body fat). This will let each individual appreciate his weight-loss accomplishment.

Have your children maintain a 1-week Walking Off Weight Calorie Record based on the number of minutes they walk that week. For each minute they log, a fat-loss credit of 5 calories can be awarded to them. At the end of the week, special awards can be made for different achievement levels.

Category	Walk Time	Calories	Fat Loss
Excellent	400 minutes	2000	0.6 pounds
Very Good	300 minutes	1500	0.45 pounds
Good	200 minutes	1000	0.3 pounds

Your New Teaching Ideas

_____

_____

_____

_____

_____

_____

_____

_____

_____

Post Graduate Workshop #10 & 11
Tobaccoless Road

A Workshop Objectives

The primary objective of these 2 workshops is to strengthen a child's commitment against tobacco—and to do so by trying to help a close friend or relative break the tobacco habit.

Students accomplish this on fresh air walks during which they identify tobacoo-users who they care enough about to want to help. Their action plan involves writing support letters to these tobacco users in which they offer assistance, understanding, and most of all love and caring to help them kick the habit. Many children receive successful responses from their letters. Some get no response. Regardless, most children become more strongly committed against tobacco as a result of this workshop.

B New Suggestions

• Take your children for a series of fresh air walks to discuss a new class project for decreasing the use of tobacco in your community and in our society in general. Use these walks to brainstorm about a creative class project aimed against tobacco. Questions to consider:

1. Could we make our school campus totally tobacco free?
2. Could we help several of our smoking teachers achieve a tobacoo-free lifestyle?
3. Could we write individual letters to our state representatives asking for support on anti-tobacco legislation?
4. Could we join hands with our local chapter of the American Lung Association on a special anti- tobacco community project?
5. Could we organize a special School Walk involving parents, teachers, and students as part of the great American Smokeout?

Post Graduate Workshop #12
Your Planet Earth

A Workshop Objectives

This workshop helps children appreciate their environment through the discoveries they make during a simple walk.

B New Suggestions

On a neighborhood walk, have your students focus on one issue that they would like to improve in their environment: (1) trash clean-up, (2) air pollution, (3) school vandalism, (4) highway traffic safety, etc. After your walk, have your students write a "walking editorial" letter to your local newspaper expressing your consensus viewpoint.

Post Graduate Workshop #13
Dealing With Stress

A Workshop Objectives

In workshop 13, students discuss their problems during a relaxing fresh air walk as a means of stress relief. The objective here is to discuss problems rather than to keep stressful feelings to ourselves. Fresh-air walking promotes conversation and helps students see that a situation may not be as bad as we sometimes believe.

B New Suggestions

One follow-up project could include a series of stress management problem-solving walks tied into the guidance counseling function. Would your guidance counselor be willing to join your class on a walk to explore a problem of mutual concern to the class. This kind of walk might even coax shy children out of their shell.

Your New Teaching Ideas

_____
_____
_____
_____
_____
_____
_____
_____
_____
_____
_____
_____
_____

Post Graduate Workshop #14
A Walk Across America

A Workshop Objectives

During the Walk Across America workshop, children learn to prioritize and work in teams as they analyze what it would be like to walk across the North American continent in a basic survival situation. Their workshop goal is to select the 10 most important items (from a list of 18 items) for their trek.

B New Suggestions

As described in Workshop 14 in **Walking for Little Children**, let your class set a year long goal to walk the 3000-mile span of North America—from Philadelphia, PA to Seattle, WA. Throughout the year, maintain a class mileage log and check your progress. Could you develop an incentive awards system for all children who make significant mileage contributions on this project? Also, could several classes race across the continent in a fun competition? Could this project be part of a geography/social studies classroom unit?
NOTE: If each student averaged about 1/2 mile per day, then your class could complete their journey in 200 schooldays!

Post Graduate Workshop #15 & #16
Self-Improvement &
Your New Walking Program

A Workshop Objectives

The goals of these two workshops are to: (1) reinforce the key principles of the Walking Wellness curriculum through a series of walking exercises, (2) measure each child's improvement in walking performance via The Straw Walk, and (3) help students develop an ongoing personal Walking Action Plan to keep them "on the road to wellness."

B New Suggestions

Self-improvement should be an ongoing effort. Every one of us, children included, should be constantly striving toward some wellness goal. Relating this to your post-graduate **Walking Wellness** program, consider the following suggestions as part of your continuing curriculum.

- Take time to individually review each student's Walking Action Plan. Were their Action Plans realistic? Did they accomplish any of their goals during the summer? Why did they succeed or fail?
- Discuss with your students (either individually or collectively) their next steps. For example, "Where do we go from here with our Action Plans? How can we keep making strides? What new Walking Wellness goals can we establish as a class? As individuals?"
- Challenge your students to come up with a creative class project for promoting class wellness. Could you develop a similar project on a schoolwide basis? Could your students propose a Wellness project that would involve *parents, teachers and school staff* and themselves?

Your New Teaching Ideas

_____
_____
_____
_____
_____
_____
_____
_____
_____
_____
_____
_____
_____
_____
_____
_____
_____
_____
_____

Walking for Little Children

A K-3 Walking Wellness Curriculum

Your success in teaching **Walking Wellness** at the elementary-middle school level will depend to a large degree on the attitudes developed by your students in early childhood. Many **Walking Wellness** teachers have commented to the effect, "I wish there was a similar walking program that could be taught at the K-1 level!"

Well, actually there is! The program is called **Walking for Little Childen**, and it is designed especially for K-3 teachers. This program is based on the philosophy that: (1) any subject can be taught on a walk, and (2) at the K-3 level, experiential learning is most critical. Consequently, in the **Walking for Little Children** program, K-3 students become involved in a whole series of educational and fitness-oriented walks. For example:

- Fitness Walks
- Little Straw Walks
- Nutrition Walks
- Snack-pack Walks
- Shadow Walks
- Bean Bag Walks
- Tunnel Walks
- Puddle Walks
- Tobaccoless Road Walks

- Nature Walks
- Alphabet Walks
- Color Walks
- Balloon Walks
- Treasure Hunt Walks
- Spelling Bee Walks
- Family Walks
- Hand-in-Hand Walks
- Grocery Walks

Aslam Amdur, kindergarten walker, demonstrating good walking posture. Fort River Elementary School.

The primary objectives of this program are to:
1. promote active walking lifestyle for ALL kids
2. promote self-esteem, honesty and respect
3. actively involve family members
4. improve children's cardiovascular fitness levels
5. promote language development & communications skills
6. promote positive wellness attitudes along with academic enrichment

The entire program is outlined in a concise teacher's resource guidebook (see following pages) called **Walking for Little Children** (64 pages with 42 photographs, 100 illustrations, charts and cartoons, and over 100 creative walking lesson plans and activities). If you are interested in obtaining more information on the **Walking for Little Children** curriculum, write or call:

Creative Walking, Inc.
P.O. Box 50296
St. Louis, MO 63105
314-721-3600

A-B-C Head Start students checking their pulse. Lame Deer, Montana.

Table of Contents

3
The Walking Teacher

The concept of adding "Walking" to your classroom curriculum may scare you at first, especially in view of all the curricula mandated these days. To look at "Walking" as one more required subject that you have to teach is a mistake. Instead, think of it as a tool to reinforce other subjects.

For instance, if you simply take your kids for 5-minute walks each day, they will learn about the colors of flowers, the movement of clouds, the sounds of nature, the flights of birds, and the fragrance of fresh air. With every walk, their vocabulary and speaking skills will increase. They will become sharper observers and better explorers. Their creativity will blossom. And in the process, your kids will be getting the physical activity necessary for good health. They may also develop a liking for exercise and movement.

On a walk, you can learn about...

History, geography, weather, nature, vegetation, science, animals

Geometric shapes, counting, addition, subtraction, fractions, estimating, logic, reasoning, space, time

Aerobics, warm-ups, posture, walking technique, pacing, strength, stretching

Listening, teamwork, cooperation, trust, friendship, sharing

Reading, spelling, vocabulary, writing, speaking

Observing, exploring, discovering, navigating, sensing, recalling

Nutrition, energy, weight control, lifestyle planning, drug-free living, relaxation

Walking, Teaching, and Learning

The human mind works better with increased blood flow and oxygen. Walking is one exercise that stimulates both the body and mind this way because it relaxes the body to inspire creative thinking. On walks, much of your teaching presentation will blossom spontaneously. Likewise, your children will bring up subjects that you are already studying in the classroom—colors, shapes,

sounds, smells, numbers and feelings. When you think about it, there is hardly a subject that cannot be touched on during a walk.

"All I keep hearing from my kids is, 'When are we gonna walk like Mrs. Johnson's class?'"

Teaching Objectives

The primary goal of **Walking for Little Children** is to help you develop a more balanced student—healthy in body as well as mind. The walking lesson plans and workshop exercises in this resource guidebook are designed to:

■ promote active walking lifestyles in a non-competitive, win-win environment by involving 100% of your class.

■ integrate health and physical education by focusing on nutrition, tobacco, drugs, stress and hygiene during walks.

■ improve communication skills, analytical reasoning and scientific understanding on walks.

■ promote honesty, respect, cooperation and teamwork.

■ help children appreciate their environment.

■ draw family members, school staff and children closer together.

■ improve the posture, endurance and the overall fitness level of each student.

■ help students create their own walking health plan.

The Student Workbook

The *Walking Wellness Student Workbook* is a multi-purpose resource book written for 4th to 8th grade children. For students, this 80-page workbook serves as their *Text*, *Journal* and *Homework Notebook*. In it students record their walking accomplishments and performances (i.e. their walking paces, heart rates, etc.), personal goals, action plans, observations and feelings. By keeping regular notes and charting their walking statistics, children learn more and retain more.

The *Student Workbook* is divided into 16 separate workshop lessons. Each workshop is arranged as a 4-page unit (see layout below) containig a wealth of health and fitness related information, motivational photographs, instructions for the workshop, data sheets for recording results, and accompanying homework assignments. The workbook's *APPENDIX* includes Walking Tips, Food Calorie Charts, an Exercise Glossary, Famous Walking Quotations and Creative Walking Ideas. As such, it like the rest of the workbook, serves as a valuable reference/resource for children and families throughout life.

WALKING
STUDENT WORKBOOK
WELLNESS

Robert Sweetgall
Robert Neeves, PhD
Exercise Physiology

The Four-Page Workshop

FIRST PAGE

Workshop title
Illustrative photo(s)
Descriptive caption

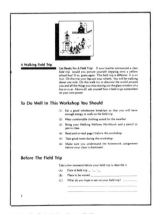

SECOND PAGE

Introduction
Objectives
Workshop Plan

THIRD PAGE

Workshop exercises
Data recording
Workshop questions
Lesson summary

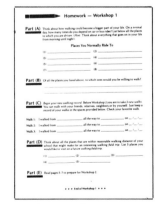

FOURTH PAGE

Homework projects
Review problems
Action Plans assignments

WALKING

STUDENT WORKBOOK

WELLNESS

Robert Sweetgall
Robert Neeves, PhD

Student	_____
School	_____
Grade	_____
Teacher	_____
Subject	_____

Published by:
Creative Walking, Inc.
P.O. Box 50296
St. Louis, MO 63105
314-721-3600

Copyright © 1987
Robert J. Sweetgall
ISBN 0-939041-04-9

Other books by Creative Walking Inc.
☐ Walking For Little Children
☐ Walking Wellness Teacher's Guide
☐ The Walker's Journal
☐ Walking Off Weight
☐ Treadmill Walking
☐ Road Scholars
☐ The NEW Teacher (newsletter)

Special Credits:
Cover design: Lynne Tesch. Artwork and layout: John Carlisle, Donna
Frommelt, and Lynn Burds, of Carlisle Communications. Illustrations: Marcia
Panych. Photography: As noted.

About the Front Cover
Students at Fort River Elementary School (Amherst, MA) find that walking is
entertaining and educational exercise as they walk with Rob Sweetgall.
Photograph by Joanne Witek.

About the Back Cover
One of the youngest "walking clubs" in America, *The Fort River Walkers*,
welcome the new weekends with *Friday Fitness Walks*.
Photograph by Joanne Witek.

Table of Contents

Acknowledgement

One morning on my walk across America, the 123rd morning of my walk, I was eating breakfast in a cattle auction cafe with Dr. Sara Jane Bates and Jim Wassom, principal and assistant principal of Oaklea Middle School (Junction City, Oregon) where I was scheduled to give an assembly program on "Walking" that morning. Over pancakes, the three of us "brainstormed" about a future Junction City parent-teacher-student community walk. Dr. Bates said: ". . . if we could only tie this walk into our school curriculum for a full year of walking education."

Walking alone on the highways, across the deserts, Rockies, Great Plains and Appalachia, I thought about that breakfast conversation. After millions of footsteps of thought, I came up with over 100 ideas to help children walk for wellness. After my walk, I rearranged those ideas into 20 workshops—a course I named *Walking Wellness.* Many of the creative ideas for these workshops were inspired by great people, especially children, whom I met along the way . . . children who joined me on the highway or near their schools for a mile or two or more of walking . . . children who provided me with good company, good conversation and kind actions. To all of you, my roadside companions, thanks for helping me finish this mission.

To the 150 Anna P. Mote Elementary School 6th graders who walked with me the opening 3½ miles from Delaware to Maryland . . . to all the Maryland students in Elkton, Westminster, Cumberland and Hagerstown who escorted me to their schools . . . to Robert of Uniontown who walked a mile with me past the fork in the road where I would have gotten lost . . . to 4th grader Shawn of Clear Springs, MD who met me in a gas station and got me to speak at her school . . . to the Toledo school bands for playing 3 miles of marching music . . . to 9-year-old David who walked 2 miles through center city Chicago telling me how he planned to walk around the world when he grew up that next year . . . to Terry Weisman's 3-year-old son who walked and piggybacked 20 miles with us . . . to St. Odelia's 400 students who walked a schoolyard lap with me . . . to Buck, 13, who walked 9 miles in freezing rain with me . . . to the Teske children who lent me their winter jackets for sleeping covers in their grocery store attic loft . . . to all 8 students of the Springdale Country Schoolhouse who let me play in their kickball game at lunch recess . . . to the 75 students of Helena and Anderson Middle Schools who walked me up the Continental Divide . . . to the Leroy children: Navarre, Charity, Dakota, Cheyenne and Noah and their English sheep dog, Argon, who let me sleep in peace under their Christmas tree in their small log cabin in the icy Cascade range . . . to all the Worcester school children from the Tatnuck and Flagg Street schools in Worcester, Massachusetts who wrote me letters while following John Dignam's weekly articles of my walk in *The Evening Gazette* . . . to the Oaklea children who toured me 2 miles around Junction City's farmlands . . . to Tammy, Nathan and David who voted "yes" at the dinner table to convince their parents to let me sleep over in their home that night in Gazelle, CA . . . to the 200 children of Castaic Junction, CA who escorted me a mile in the rain to their school . . . to the boys in the Mojave Desert gas station who let me sleep in the back of their broken down Pontiac station wagon . . . to little Joseph who had his mother, Lupe, stop in the Johnson Canyon desert (UT) to see if I needed water . . . to Derrick, 12, and Patricia, 10, who each walked with me from their school in Pine Bluffs, WY to their homes in Bushnell, NE, 9.4 miles . . . to Shawn, 13, who walked 32 miles in a day with me along the Massachusetts coast . . . to my cousins Craig, Bonnie and Cindy who walked 3 miles in New York with me . . . to the new 6th graders of Mote Elementary school who traveled to New York to finish the journey their upper classmates had started with me 11,208 miles back up the road . . . to The Rockport Company and Gore-Tex Fabrics who protected my feet and body all through this walk . . . and to everyone else who helped, thank you for being so supportive. I hope you will remember walking with me as long as I will remember walking with you. Be well and keep walking. ★ ★ ★

On The Road to Wellness

Reason To Walk

Walking, any kind of walking, *fast or slow, long* or *short*, whatever, is *healthy*. In fact, *walking* is *your healthiest exercise* because you can do it for the rest of your life, safely. After all, how many senior citizens do you see playing basketball, touch football or doing aerobic dances? These sports may seem exciting to you now, but they are *not* the answer to lifelong wellness. *Walking* is the *one* exercise that is totally aerobic. It conditions the heart muscle while toning the large muscle groups (legs). Walking is energizing, entertaining and emotionally rewarding. It promotes creative thinking, relieves stress and improves the quality of sleep. Walking burns *five times* more calories than watching TV (5 *vs.* 1 calorie per minute) to help you *lose* or *control* weight. Walking does all this and more—without high risk of injury. What other form of exercise offers you this for your whole life, and for free?

What is *Walking Wellness?*

Walking Wellness is a creative course consisting of 16 walking workshops that will exercise your mind as well as your body. During each workshop you will *walk, talk, write, read, reason, calculate, plan, cooperate* and *discover*. You will learn the meaning of *aerobic walking* and *what it is to walk* 3½ or 4 miles per hour. You will discover how fit you are by how far you can walk in 15 minutes. You will have the opportunity to plan a fitness walking program that will strengthen your heart and tone your muscles and improve your walking performance. In most workshops you will get to *walk in teams*—not in *competition*—but rather in *cooperation*. In the *Walking Calories* workshop, you and your teammates will figure out how far you need to walk to burn off a slice of apple or a piece of candy. By the end of this school year, you will have a better understanding of your body, and how to keep it healthy for the rest of your life.

Objectives

The objectives of *Walking Wellness* are:

1. To gain an appreciation of walking as both a *physical* and *mental* excercise

2. To teach you *aerobic walking* as a *lifelong, noncompetitive* exercise

3. To help you understand the relationship between *walking* and *calories* and the *food-energy balance*

4. To strengthen your commitment against tobacco

5. To use *walking* to reinforce the basic skills of *reading, writing, mathematics, and communications.*

6. To broaden your understanding of your own environment by walking in it

7. To improve your lifestyle by writing your own *Walking Wellness Action Plan*

8. To involve your family in your *Walking Wellness* assignments and lifestyle plans.

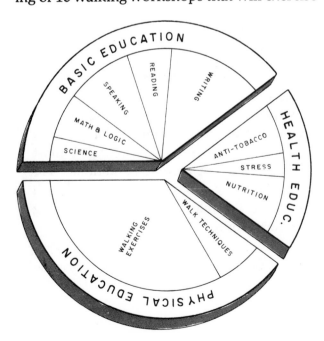

Balanced Education

How *Walking Wellness* Works

Walking Wellness is a collection of 16 workshops. On the average, you will participate in *one workshop* each week. At the beginning of each class, your teacher will explain the workshop to you. Despite this, it is a good idea to have read the workshop as part of your previous homework assignment. That way you will be familiar with the lesson of the day. In other words, as part of your homework for *Workshop 6*, it would be wise to read *Workshop 7* in your *Student Workbook*.

You will have approximately ½ hour to complete each workshop in class. Half of that time is devoted to various *walking exercises*—the other half to understanding those exercises. Each workshop is coordinated with a homework assignment which reinforces the principles of your last workshop. All assignments and instructions are completely outlined in your *Student Workbook*.

The Student Workbook

This *workbook* is yours for life. So treat it well! Let it be your *walking journal*, your *walking textbook*, your *note taking book*,

and your *homework notebook*. You must bring this workbook to all your *Walking Wellness* classes.

How To Do Well In Walking Wellness

In this course anyone can do well with some effort. You need *not* be athletic to do well in *Walking Wellness*. The important things are that you: (1) *listen to instructions from your teacher*, (2) *follow those instructions*, (3) *respect your fellow classmates*, (4) *do your Walking Wellness homework assignments*, and (5) *make positive improvements in your lifestyle*. That is all you need to do to be a *grade "A"* student in this course. Consider one other point: in *Walking Wellness* an "A" is more than just an outstanding grade. An "A" means you will probably live a longer, healthier and a happier life, and maybe that's as important as anything else on your report card.

Note 1: Brisk walking burns about the same number of calories mile for mile as jogging—but without the high impact stress placed on the joints as in jogging. Walking, with ⅓ the impact landing of jogging, creates just the right amount of stress to help your bones grow strong.

Note 2: The 3 components of a sound fitness program are: **cardiorespiratory training** (aerobics), **flexibility training** (stretching), and **strength training**. While walking helps you in all 3 of these areas, it is most beneficial as an aerobic conditioner. For this reason, walking should be used with separate flexibility and strength training exercises for total fitness.

A Walking Field Trip

Sixth grade students from the Mote Elementary School (Wilmington, DE) started an 11,208 mile walk with Rob Sweetgall on September 7, 1984. All 150 students walked with Rob 3.5 miles from Newark, DE to the Maryland State Line to kick off Rob's 50-state (Alaska and Hawaii by air shuttle), one-year solo walk of America to promote *Walking For Cardiovascular Health.* Could you walk 3.5 miles?

Photo by DuPont Magazine.

1

A Walking Field Trip

Get Ready For A Field Trip! If your teacher announced a *class field trip*, would you picture yourself stepping onto a yellow school bus? If so, guess again. This field trip is different. It is *on foot*. On this trip your legs are your wheels. You will be walking about *one mile*. On this walk try to discover the world around you and all the things you miss staring out the glass window of a bus or a car. Above all, ask yourself how it feels to go somewhere on your own power.

To Do Well In This Workshop You Should

(1) Eat a good wholesome breakfast so that you will have enough energy to walk on the field trip.

(2) Wear comfortable clothing suited for the weather.

(3) Bring your *Walking Wellness Workbook* and a pencil or pen to class.

(4) Read and re-read page 3 *before* this workshop.

(5) Take good notes during this workshop.

(6) Make sure you understand the homework assignment before your class is dismissed.

Before The Field Trip

Take a few moments before your field trip to describe it.

(A) Date of field trip __ / __ / __

(B) Place to be visited _____

(C) What do you hope to see on your field trip? _____

_____

_____

Questions To Think About

During your field trip take time to write down your thoughts to questions below.

Question 1 What scenery have you noticed while walking that you never noticed before from a car?

_____

_____

Question 2 What was your favorite part of this walk?

_____

_____

Question 3 What did you learn on this walk?

_____

_____

Question 4 How does going somewhere on foot make you feel inside?

_____

_____

Question 5 What new ideas came into your mind on your walk?

_____

_____

After The Field Trip

After you return to school, take a few minutes to finish answering the 5 questions above. Then use the space below to write down comments made by your classmates. If you take good notes, your homework will be easier.

_____

_____

_____

about how walking could become a bigger part of your life. On a normal
w many times do you depend on car or bus rides? List below all the places
h you are *driven*. (*Hint:* Think about everything that goes on in your life
orning until night).

Places You Normally Ride To

(1) _____ (2) _____

(3) _____ (4) _____

(5) _____ (6) _____

(7) _____ (8) _____

Part (B)

Of all the places you listed above, to which ones would you be willing to walk?

_____

_____

Part (C)

Begin your new walking record. Before Workshop 2 you are to take 3 *new walks.*
You can walk with your friends, relatives, neighbors or by yourself. Just keep a
record of your walks in the spaces provided below. Check your favorite walk.

Walk 1: I walked from _____ all the way to _____ on __ / __ / __.

Walk 2: I walked from _____ all the way to _____ on __ / __ / __.

Walk 3: I walked from _____ all the way to _____ on __ / __ / __.

Part (D)

Think about all the places that are within reasonable walking distance of your
school that might make for an interesting *walking field trip*. List 5 places you
would like to visit on a future *walking field trip*.

(1) _____ (2) _____ (3) _____

(4) _____ (5) _____

Part (E)

Read pages 5–7 to prepare for Workshop 2.

Aerobic Walking

Photo by Joe Forward, Oaklea Middle School.

An easy way to measure your pulse: Immediately following your walking exercise, gently place your 2nd and 3rd fingers on your carotid artery (side of neck). Count the number of pulses in 6 *seconds*. Multiply that number by 10 to find your heart rate (*beats per minute*). For example: If you count 8 beats in 6 seconds, your *pulse* is 8 × 10 or 80 beats per minute (BPM). If you count 12, then your *pulse* is 12 × 10 or 120.

For the majority of children, aerobic walking is highly beneficial if it raises the heart rate between 120 and 150 beats per minute (12 to 15 pulses during a 6 second count). How fast does your heart beat when you walk?

Aerobic Walking

Let's Walk Aerobically! Walking is one of the best all-around aerobic exercises. It can help you lose weight. It strengthens your heart and tones your other muscles. Walking can help you control stress, and it will improve your mental alertness and creativity. Besides, walking is the *safest* exercise.

In your first workshop you took *A Walking Field Trip*. Can you remember how easy a walk that was? You might even wonder if such *easy walking* is "real exercise." Actually it is! Yes, even *easy walking* is exercise. However, *brisk* (fast) *walking* will benefit you more. The ideal walking pace is that pace which *you can maintain for 20 to 40 straight minutes without pain*. During a fast walk your heart beats faster—typically 120 to 150 times per minute. Your breathing speeds up too, but not so much that you become winded. This is aerobic walking.

Your Walking Goal

In this *Aerobic Walking workshop* your goal is to discover the walking speed which raises your heart rate **above 120** beats per minute, but **not above 150** beats per minute. This can be accomplished by measuring your *pulse* immediately after each of your walks. If your pulse is **below 120,** you can walk faster. If your pulse is **above 150,** you may need to slow down. If your heart is beating between 120 and 150 times per minute, then you have found the *aerobic target zone*.

This whole process is a *trial & error* technique. You *try* one pace and check your heart rate. Then you *try* a new walking pace and check again. Eventually you will hit your target heart rate.

6

Trial Walk 1

Your First Aerobic Walk   In Trial 1 your teacher will pace you around the *Straw Walk* course at a comfortable pace of 3.5 MPH.

As you begin your first lap, note your breathing level and the amount of effort required to walk 3.5 MPH. Can you sense how fast your heart is beating? Are you breaking a sweat? Is your body warming up?

As you finish your lap, wait for your teacher's signal so you can measure your *pulse*. This will tell you your *walking heart rate* which you should record along with your *lap time* below. You can find your *pace* by using the *walking speed tables* in the appendix of this book (page 85).

Aerobic Walk	Lap Time	Pace	Walking Heart Rate (Pulse)
Trial 1	____:____(min:sec)	____.____MPH	_____Beats/Min (BPM)
Trial 2	____:____(min:sec)	____.____MPH	_____Beats/Min (BPM)
Trial 3	____:____(min:sec)	____.____MPH	_____Beats/Min (BPM)

Trial Walk 2

Adjusting Your Pace   You are now on your own! Your teacher will not pace you for this lap. Now you must decide whether to walk *faster* or *slower* than in Trial 1. Your decision should be based on *your walking heart rate (pulse)* as measured in Trial 1. If your *pulse* was **below 120,** then you need to walk *faster.* If your pulse was **above 150,** you need to walk *slower.*

Trial Walk 3

Your Final Adjustment   Walk *faster* or *slower* such that your *heart beat (pulse)* falls in the *aerobic target zone* (120 to 150 BPM). Again, *record* your *lap time* and *pulse.*

Physical Feelings   In the space below, briefly describe how you feel after walking aerobically.

_____

_____

_____

Part (A) For the 4 activities listed below, guess what your *heart rate* will be. Record your estimates below.

Activity	Part (A) Your Estimated Heart Rate (BPM)	Part (B) Your Measured Heart Rate (BPM)	Part (C) Aerobic Zone
Lying Still in Bed	_____	_____	_____
After Brushing Your Teeth	_____	_____	_____
After Climbing 1 Flight of Stairs	_____	_____	_____
After a 16 Minute Brisk Walk	_____	_____	_____

Part (B) Perform each of the 4 activities above (separately of course). Then immediately following each activity, measure your pulse. Record your pulse alongside your estimates. How close were your guesses?

Part (C) In the column marked **Aerobic Zone,** place a check next to those activities you feel were good aerobic exercises. In the space below, describe the kind of physical feelings you get that let you know when you are exercising in the *aerobic target zone.*

_____

_____

_____

_____

_____

Part (D) Read pages 9–11 to prepare for Workshop 3.

The Straw Walk

In a *Straw Walk*, the object is to walk ¼ mile laps at the fastest pace you can hold for a *full 15 minutes.* The fitter you become, the more laps you will be able to walk in 15 minutes. As you complete each lap you will be handed a "straw." The trick is to keep moving in stride as your teacher hands you your "straw." How many "straws" could you earn in 15 minutes of fast walking?

Photo by Joe Forward, Oaklea M. S., Junction City, OR.

Photo by Joanne Witek, Fort River Elementary, Amherst, MA.

The Straw Walk

How Fast Can You Walk?   How many laps of a ¼ mile loop can you walk in 15 straight minutes? 3 laps? 3½ laps? How about 4 laps (1 mile)? Or are you in good enough shape to walk 5 laps in 15 minutes? You will find out in the *Straw Walk* that follows!

What Is A Straw Walk?

A *Straw Walk* is a 15-minute fast walk. How fast is fast? Here *fast* means the *fastest walking pace* you can hold for *15 full minutes.*

Why Do The Straw Walk?

The *Straw Walk* helps you *four different ways:* (1) It tells you how *fit* you are. (2) It teaches you *pacing.* (3) It tells you your walking *speed.* (4) It provides you with great aerobic exercise. All this is accomplished in 15 minutes.

To Do Well In A Straw Walk You Should

(1)   Save your breath by *not* talking.

(2)   Walk at your own pace—*not* your friend's pace.

(3)   Warm up slowly before your *Straw Walk.*

(4)   Pace yourself so you do not "burn-out."

(5)   Avoid eating a large meal right before the walk.

(6)   Avoid slowing down for your straw hand-off.

   Important: this is a walk—not a run. Also, the *Straw Walk* is ***not*** a test. This is an exercise that will help you determine your *fitness level.* If you *jog* or *run* during the *Straw Walk,* you are only cheating *yourself!*

Your First
Straw Walk

Assemble at the *start line* of the *Straw Walk* course and quietly listen for instructions. Try to *relax!* When your teacher gives a signal, begin walking fast. Each time you complete *one lap,* make sure you receive a straw. After 15 minutes a *whistle* will sound. *Freeze* in place and prepare to take your pulse. Count your heartbeats starting with the next whistle (2nd whistle) and ending 6 seconds later (3rd whistle). *Record your heart rate and Straw Walk score* below. Then as your teacher comes by, announce your *score,* hand over your straws, and continue your cool–down walk.

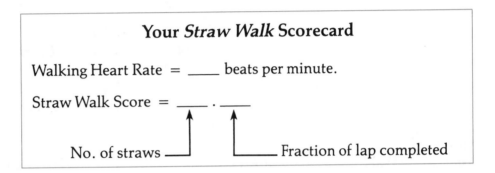

Example

Your Straw Walk Score   is the number of laps you completed . . . plus . . . your position on the course as of the final whistle. For example, if you finished with 4 straws, at the 6th cone on the Straw Walk Course, then your Straw Walk Score is 4.6 (4 and 6/10 laps). That means you averaged 4.6 MPH for 15 full minutes.

Improving Your
Straw Walks

How Fit Are You?   Look at your **Straw Walk Score** above. Now examine the chart on page 12. Where do you stand on the Fitness Scale?

Question: Why is the **Straw Walk** a good measure of cardio-vascular fitness?

Answer: The fitter you are, the further you will be able to walk in 15 minutes.

Straw Walk Fitness Scale

	Straw Walk Score	Fitness Percentile		Straw Walk Score	Fitness Percentile
Excellent	5.4	99%	Fair	3.9	65%
	5.3	98%		3.8	60%
	5.2	97%		3.7	55%
	5.1	96%		3.6	50%
	5.0	95%		3.5	45%
Very Good	4.9	93%	Not So Good	3.4	40%
	4.8	90%		3.3	32%
	4.7	88%		3.2	24%
	4.6	85%		3.1	16%
	4.5	82%		3.0	10%
Good	4.4	80%			
	4.3	77%			
	4.2	75%			
	4.1	73%			
	4.0	70%			

Example: If you can score 4.8 for example, you will be in the top 10% (90th percentile) of all American children walking.

How to Improve Your Straw Walk

Study the High and Low Performance Factors to the right. Which Low Performance Factors in your lifestyle could you improve on?

Low Performance Factors:

Pacing unevenly
Talking while walking
Walking with arms at your side
Walking with hunched-over posture
Being overweight
Watching too much TV
Being too tense
Poor endurance training
Using tobacco
Eating fatty/junk foods

For High Performance:

Maintain a steady pace
Save your "wind" for breathing
Swing your arms to and fro
Walk tall
Trim down
Be more physically active
Relax on the walk
Practice longer walks
Avoid tobacco
Eat a balanced high-carbohydrate diet

Your Second *Straw Walk*

Do you think that you can improve on your first *Straw Walk* Score? Remember, to do well in the *Straw Walk*: (1) relax at the start, (2) pace yourself from the beginning, (3) swing your arms, (4) avoid conversation, (5) stay on the inside lane and (6) give yourself an easy walking warm-up and cool-down.

Comparing Your Straw Walk Scores

First Straw Walk Score = ____.____   Heart Rate = ____ bpm

Second Straw Walk Score = ____.____   Heart Rate = ____ bpm

Straw Walk Mathematics

To calculate your *Straw Walk* score, *add* together the number of straws you collected in 15 minutes (Column 1) *and* the fraction of the last lap you completed (Column 2). The sum is your *Straw Walk* score (Column 3) which also tells you your average walking speed (Column 4) in *miles per hour*. Columns 5 & 6 tell you *how long* it would take you to walk ¼ mile and 1 mile, respectively.

(Column 1) No. Straws In Hand	(Column 2) The Tenth Marker Closest To Where You Finished	(Column 3) Straw Walk Score	(Column 4) Average Walking Speed	(Column 5) ¼ Mi. Time (1 Lap) (min:sec)	(Column 6) 1 Mi. Time (4 Laps) (min:sec)
3 Straws	$^0/_{10}$	3.0	3.0 MPH	5:00	20:00
3 Straws	$^1/_{10}$	3.1	3.1 MPH	4:50	19:20
3 Straws	$^2/_{10}$	3.2	3.2 MPH	4:41	18:45
3 Straws	$^3/_{10}$	3.3	3.3 MPH	4:32	18:10
3 Straws	$^4/_{10}$	3.4	3.4 MPH	4:25	17:40
3 Straws	$^5/_{10}$	3.5	3.5 MPH	4:17	17:08
3 Straws	$^6/_{10}$	3.6	3.6 MPH	4:10	16:40
3 Straws	$^7/_{10}$	3.7	3.7 MPH	4:03	16:12
3 Straws	$^8/_{10}$	3.8	3.8 MPH	3:56	15:46
3 Straws	$^9/_{10}$	3.9	3.9 MPH	3:50	15:22
4 Straws	$^0/_{10}$	4.0	4.0 MPH	3:45	15:00
4 Straws	$^1/_{10}$	4.1	4.1 MPH	3:40	14:38
4 Straws	$^2/_{10}$	4.2	4.2 MPH	3:34	14:16
4 Straws	$^3/_{10}$	4.3	4.3 MPH	3:29	13:57
4 Straws	$^4/_{10}$	4.4	4.4 MPH	3:24	13:37
4 Straws	$^5/_{10}$	4.5	4.5 MPH	3:20	13:20
4 Straws	$^6/_{10}$	4.6	4.6 MPH	3:15	13:02
4 Straws	$^7/_{10}$	4.7	4.7 MPH	3:12	12:45
4 Straws	$^8/_{10}$	4.8	4.8 MPH	3:07	12:30
4 Straws	$^9/_{10}$	4.9	4.9 MPH	3:03	12:15
5 Straws	$^0/_{10}$	5.0	5.0 MPH	3:00	12:00
5 Straws	$^1/_{10}$	5.1	5.1 MPH	2:56	11:45
5 Straws	$^2/_{10}$	5.2	5.2 MPH	2:53	11:32
5 Straws	$^3/_{10}$	5.3	5.3 MPH	2:50	11:20
5 Straws	$^4/_{10}$	5.4	5.4 MPH	2:46	11:07
5 Straws	$^5/_{10}$	5.5	5.5 MPH	2:43	10:55
5 Straws	$^6/_{10}$	5.6	5.6 MPH	2:40	10:42
5 Straws	$^7/_{10}$	5.7	5.7 MPH	2:38	10:32
5 Straws	$^8/_{10}$	5.8	5.8 MPH	2:35	10:20
5 Straws	$^9/_{10}$	5.9	5.9 MPH	2:32	10:10
6 Straws	$^0/_{10}$	6.0	6.0 MPH	2:30	10:00

Comparing Your Two Straw Walks

Part (A) Answer the following questions.

Question 1   Did your *Straw Walk* score improve? _____ YES _____ NO. If you answered YES, what factor(s) do you think made the biggest difference?

_____

_____

_____

Question 2   *Setting Your New Fitness Walking Goal.* Turn back to page 12 and compare your **Two** straw walk scores to the **Straw Walk Fitness Scale.** Now ask yourself: "What percentile rank and Straw Walk Score would I like to achieve by the end of this Walking Wellness course?" Enter your goal below:

My goal is to reach ____.____ for a Straw Walk score which would rank me at the ____ percentile level for all school children in America.

Question 3   *Improve Your Straw Walk Score.* Study the *high* and *low performance factors* shown on page 12. Then think about your health habits and your walking program. What specific steps will you take to achieve your new Straw Walk goal?

Step (1) _____

Step (2) _____

Step (3) _____

Step (4) _____

Part (B): Read pages 15–17 to prepare for Workshop 4.

Teamwalks

The art of teamwork: This team of students at Fort River Elementary School is trying to figure out whether they need to slow down or speed up to average 3.5 mph during their *Teamwalk*. Are they listening to each other well? Do you know how to walk 3.5 mph?

Photo by Fort River Elementary School.

Teamwalk

How Fast Is a 3.5 MPH Walk? If someone walked up to you and said: "Show me how to walk three and a half miles in one hour," what would you do? By the end of this *Teamwalk* workshop you should be able to show anyone how to walk 3.5 MPH!

Why is 3.5 MPH Walking Important?

Would you believe 3.5 MPH walking is the most *practical* type of walking for nearly everyone? Why? At 3.5 MPH, most people can walk long distances without tiring or getting sore muscles. It is a great pace for hiking or walking to school or getting around without becoming exhausted or out of breath. A 3.5 MPH walk is a comfortable pace, yet it is still good enough to qualify as *aerobic exercise* . . . and without the sweat too!

Working in Teams

Besides learning how to walk 3.5 MPH, this workshop teaches you the importance of *teamwork.* Good *teamwork* takes good *listening.* To do well in this workshop, you will need to cooperate and listen to your teammates.

Your New Team The colored card that your teacher hands you will tell you your team: **Red . . . Orange . . . Yellow . . . Green . . . Blue.** As soon as you find out your team color, move to your team position as shown below.

**Team Formations:
Lining up on
the Straw Walk Course**

Blue Team	Green Team	Orange Team	Yellow Team	Red Team
☺ ☺	☺ ☺	☺ ☺	☺ ☺	☺ ☺
☺ ☺	☺ ☺	☺ ☺	☺ ☺	☺ ☺
☺ ☺	☺ ☺	☺ ☺	☺ ☺	☺ ☺

 STRAW WALK COURSE Start Line

16

Your Team Goal Your team goal is to walk *one lap* of the *Straw Walk* course at a 3.5 MPH pace! The "trick" is to cooperate as a team to figure out the perfect pace. The whole idea is to keep discussing your pace as you walk.

"Are we going too fast for 3.5 MPH?" . . . "Too slow?" . . . "Or are we right on target?" Remember, your team must stick together as a unit!

Keeping Score All team members should keep their own score. First begin by recording your *start time*. When you complete your lap, record your *finish time*. Subtract your *start time from your finish time* to find *your lap time*.

The **Teamwalk**: 3.5 miles per hour. *

* a perfect score is a 4 minute, 17 second lap.

Lap 1 ⟶ Start Time ____ : ____   Finish Time ____ : ____   Lap Time ____ : ____

Lap 2 ⟶ Start Time ____ : ____   Finish Time ____ : ____   Lap Time ____ : ____

After Finishing Lap 1 Immediately calculate your *lap time* and huddle as a team to discuss your *team performance*. (1) How can you improve as a team? _____
(2) Was everyone heard, or did anyone feel left out? _____
(3) Be prepared for your second 3.5 MPH Teamwalk!

Doing the Teamwalk at 4.0 miles per hour

In the 3.5 MPH Teamwalk (above), you discovered the feeling of walking at a 17 minute-per-mile pace. You also learned about team communications. Now you will have a chance to apply your learning in a more challenging walk at 4 MPH. This means you will need to "shave" 32 seconds off your 3.5 MPH lap time to maintain a 4 MPH pace on the Straw Walk course. As you walk, think about how much more energy is required to walk at a 15 minute-per-mile pace. Once again, keep up the great teamwork and record your scores for each lap (1 and 2) below.

The **Teamwalk**: 4.0 miles per hour. *

* a perfect score is a 3 minute, 45 second lap.

Lap 1   Start Time ____ : ____   Finish Time ____ : ____   Lap Time ____ : ____

Lap 2   Start Time ____ : ____   Finish Time ____ : ____   Lap Time ____ : ____

After Finishing Lap 2 After recording your *lap time*, huddle as a team to discuss your performance. Start discussing **Part A** of your homework.

▶ Homework — Workshop 4

Part (A)
Answer each question below in the space provided.

(1) In both the 3.5 and 4.0 MPH Teamwalk, did your team do better on its second attempt (Lap 2)?_____ . If so, why? _____ .

_____

(2) How did you compromise when there was disagreement about how fast to walk?

_____

(3) Did you personally feel that you had a "say" in how fast your team walked? ____ YES ____ NO. How many times each lap were you responsible for changing the pace? Did you listen to others on your team? ____ YES ____ NO.

(4) If you could do this exercise again, what would you do differently to help your team?

_____

Part (B)
Circle the best answer to each question below.

(5) The purpose of this *Teamwalk* workshop was:

    (a) To learn how to walk 3.5 MPH and 4.0 MPH.
    (b) To see how fast you could walk.
    (c) To learn to work in a group.
    (d) To do better than the other team.
    (e) Both (a) and (c) above.

(6) You probably felt part of your team if:

    (a) You had some say in determining pace.
    (b) You listened to others.
    (c) Everyone on your team did their own thing.
    (d) You controlled everything.
    (e) Both (a) and (b) above.

Part (C)
List below the difference that you felt walking at 3.5 MPH versus 4.0 MPH :

At 3.5 MPH, I felt _____

At 4.0 MPH, I felt _____

Part (D)
Read pages 19–23 to prepare for Workshop 5.

★ ★ ★ **End of Workshop 4** ★ ★ ★

Walking in Rhythm

Good *Arm Swing* gives your body a natural walking rhythm and sense of balance. With this you can walk longer distances without tiring. Your arm swing will also give your upper body muscles a good workout.

Which students are letting their arms swing freely to help balance their walking stride? Judging from *left* to *right:* 1st student is good, but left arm could be in closer to body; 2nd and 3rd students are very good; 4th student is good, but head could be more upright; 5th, 6th and 7th students are good; 8th student is good, considering he is turning around to talk.

Walking in Rhythm

Natural Walking   Walking is natural. Is it not? You know how to walk. You swing your arms forward and backwards, and step along. What could be simpler? It's like breathing; you hardly have to think about it. You just do it. It just happens.

Why Swing Your Arms When Walking?   Yet there is more to walking than we might think . . . the way our legs move with each arm swing. Right arm forward—right leg back; left arm forward—left leg back. Heel, toe, . . . heel, toe. Right, left . . . right, left. With each step your arms swing like the pendulum of a grandfather clock. What does this *arm swing* do for us? First, it helps us balance our bodies. Actually it's like walking a tight-rope with a balance bar. Take away that balance bar from the tightrope walker, and all of a sudden his body starts shaking and swaying. The arms are really a walker's balance bar. Besides providing balance, your arm swing sets the timing of your step. The faster your arms swing—the faster your step. With this motion more power is added to your walking stride.

In summary, *swinging your arms* helps you by:

(1) Improving your *balance*
(2) Setting your *timing* and *rhythm*
(3) Adding to your *power*
(4) Reducing your fatigue

Walking in Rhythm   In this workshop you will be experimenting with *3 different walking motions during 3 separate walks:*

(1) *No arm swing walk* (hands clasped in front or in back of you)
(2) *Easy arm swing walk* (arms swing naturally at your side)
(3) *High-energy arm swing walk* (arms swing fast and forcefully)

During each of these 3 walks you are to keep score of your lap times, so you can compare the difference *arm swing* makes in walking performance. Record your *lap times* for each style.

Walk 1

The no arm swing walk As you line up to start your lap of the *Straw Walk* course, practice walking a few steps with your *workbooks* held directly *in front* or directly *in back* of you. Clutch your *workbook* with *both hands.* This will prevent arm swing during this lap. It may feel a bit awkward and uncomfortable walking this way, but this will show you the value of a good arm swing.

For *one full lap* walk as fast as possible, but keep holding your workbook with *two hands.* As you complete your lap, listen for your *lap time* and record it on the *Walking In Rhythm* scorecard below. Following each lap, also record how that particular style of walking felt to you.

Walking in Rhythm

Walk #	Walk Description	¼ Mile Lap Time (minutes:seconds)	Walker's Comments
Walk 1	No arm swing	___:___	_____
Walk 2	Easy arm swing	___:___	_____
Walk 3	High-energy arm swing	___:___	_____

Walk 2

The easy arm swing walk Walk a second lap, but this time hold your *workbook* in one hand and let your arms swing freely at your side. Again, walk as *fast* as you comfortably can. Record your *lap time* and *comments* once more.

What differences did you notice between the **no arm swing walk** (1) and the **easy arm swing walk** (2)?

_____

_____

Walk 3

The high-energy, arm swing walk This time walk one lap as *fast* as possible with your arms swinging *rapidly with high-energy* at your sides. Record your *lap time* and *comments* on finishing. Was Walk 3 your fastest walk? ____YES ____NO

What was the biggest difference in how you felt in Walk 1 versus Walk 2 versus Walk 3?

_____

_____

_____

Homework — Workshop 5

Part (A) Compare your *lap times* in Walks 1, 2 and 3. Did you walk faster when you swung your arms at your sides? _____ YES _____ NO. Why do you think swinging your arms helps you walk better?

_____

_____

Part (B) This week in your neighborhood or at your school, take time out to observe 3 people who are walking. From a fair distance watch how they swing their arms. On the chart below describe their *arm swing* and *how they might improve.*

	Describe Arm Swing	**Room For Improvement**
Walker 1	_____	_____
Walker 2	_____	_____
Walker 3	_____	_____

Part (C) Answer TRUE or FALSE for each of the statements below by checking the appropriate space.

(1) _____ TRUE _____ FALSE Proper arm swing adds *rhythm* and *timing*, *balance* and *power* to the walking stride.

(2) _____ TRUE _____ FALSE As your left arm swings forward while walking, your left foot moves forward, too.

(3) _____ TRUE _____ FALSE If it took you 800 *right footsetps* and 800 *left footsteps* to walk 1 mile, then your *right and left* arms probably swung forward about 800 times each during that mile walk.

(4) _____ TRUE _____ FALSE Assume your *Straw Walk* score was 3.7 without hardly any arm-swing action in your walk. If you increased your arm-swing energy, you would expect your *Straw Walk* score to increase.

(5) _____ TRUE _____ FALSE As you swing your arms faster and harder on a walk, it is likely that your walking heart rate will decrease.

Part (D) Read pages 23–26 to prepare for Workshop 6.

Posture Walk

Your *walking posture* speaks for you. It's your body language. A great way to improve your posture is to have someone observe you as you walk. That person can offer you the kind of constructive criticism you cannot get by looking in a mirror. What makes for good walking posture? How is your walking posture?

Photo by Joe Forward, Oaklea Middle School.

Posture Walk

How's Your Body Language? The way you walk is the way your body talks. Your walking posture is a form of body language. Walking slouched or bent over conveys a *low-energy, dull, depressed, sad* mood. On the other hand, walking upright with head focused straight ahead conveys a positive, alert, and upbeat mood. People read you by your walking posture. So why give off *negative vibrations.* Walk with good posture, and let people see the best in you!

Good Posture Makes a Good Walker Walking posture does more than convey your image and tell your story. It affects your walking performance. People with poor posture tire faster. They walk slower, and their muscles become sore easily. They also walk inefficiently, wasting energy. The *good news* is that we can all *improve* our walking posture. All we need to do is practice the *Six Posture Pointers.*

Points of Posture

What makes for good walking posture? Here are 6 basic posture pointers which will help tune-up your *walking machine.*

Pointer 1 Walk with your head level—*not* up, *not* down, *not* off to either side—just straight ahead. You should be able to balance a book on your head while walking.

Pointer 2 Walk with level shoulders and a level trunk—not like the Leaning Tower of Pisa.

Pointer 3 Swing your arms front to back with your elbows in close to your sides.

Pointer 4 Walk *tall!* Keep an erect posture with a straight back. Avoid slouching like an ape.

Pointer 5 Point your feet straight ahead in the direction of travel as if walking a balance beam.

Pointer 6 With each footstep, land on your heel . . . then roll on the ball of your foot . . . and push off on your toes. This is called *heel-toe walking.*

Walking With a "Buddy" Split into teams of 2 by picking a *walking buddy*. While one of you walks (*the walker*), the other will walk alongside and observe (*the observer*).

Hint For the Walker: Just walk naturally. **Hint for the Observer:** Check out your buddy from all angles . . . front, back, side. Record your observations below.

	Name of Walker _____	Name of Observer _____
1st Half	1 Head level? _____	4 Body tall and erect? _____
of Posture	2 Shoulders level? _____	5 Feet straight ahead? _____
Walk 1	3 Arm swing straight? _____	6 Heel-toe action? _____

Halfway around the *Straw Walk* course you and your buddy should *stop!* *The observer* must critique *the walker's* posture. Both of you should take notes (use chart above). Now *the walker* becomes *the observer* and vice versa for the last half of Lap 1. On finishing Lap 1, *the observer* should comment. Both of you are to take notes below.

	Name of Walker _____	Name of Observer _____
2nd Half	1 Head level? _____	4 Body tall and erect? _____
of Posture	2 Shoulders level? _____	5 Feet straight ahead? _____
Walk 1	3 Arm swing straight? _____	6 Heel-toe action? _____

Posture Walk 2 In *Posture Walk 2*, you will walk with your same buddy. Repeat your roles as *walker* and *observer*. *This time focus on improvement.* As in Lap 1, STOP at the halfway point to take notes and critique. Then switch roles.

Did your buddy really improve? Be honest! Write your comments here. _____

Did your posture improve in the second walk? Write your buddy's comments here. _____

Posture Walk 3 Think about what you have learned about *your posture*. Now, can you apply this to improve your walking? Your goal is to set a new personal record by walking your *fastest lap* by improving on just one point of your posture.

Posture walk 3 lap time = ____:____(minutes:seconds)
Best lap time from Workshop 5 (page 21) = ____:____

Final Questions Did changing your posture improve your walking performance? _____ If so, how?_____

_____

Homework — Workshop 6

Part (A) It is impossible to be your own walking judge because you cannot see yourself walking. That is why it is good to have someone else observe your walking posture. In school that *someone else* was your *buddy (the observer)*. Hopefully your *buddy* helped you, but it never hurts to get a second opinion.

For homework you are to continue your *Posture Walk*, but with a new partner. Your new partner can be your mother, father, another relative, friend, or teacher. Follow the same rules as in Workshop 6 by switching roles as *walker* and *observer*.

Before starting your *Posture Walk*, teach your new partner the *six basic pointers of good walking posture* (page 24). For the *first half* of your walk you should play *the observer*. After a few minutes of walking, explain your observations to your partner. Write everything down below. Then let your partner observe you walk. Again, after stopping, write down your partner's observations.

My Observation of _____

1 Head level? _____
2 Shoulders level? _____
3 Arm swing straight? _____
4 Body tall and erect? _____
5 Feet straight ahead? _____
6 Heel-toe action? _____

My partner's observation of me

1 Head level? _____
2 Shoulders level? _____
3 Arm swing straight? _____
4 Body tall and erect? _____
5 Feet straight ahead? _____
6 Heel-toe action? _____

Question 1 What things did your new partner tell you that were not mentioned by your buddy in school?

_____

_____

_____

Question 2 After all these *Posture Walks*, what is the *one point of posture* that you need to practice the most?

_____

_____

_____

Part (B) Read pages 27–30 to prepare for Workshop 7.

End of Workshop 6

Walking Calories

Photo by Fort River Elementary School, Amherst, MA.

How long would you need to walk to burn off the calories contained in a carrot stick? That is what these children are discovering as they try to figure out what fraction of the *Straw Walk* loop they need to walk to burn off a carrot. If you were on *The Carrot Team*, how far would you walk to burn off a carrot?

Note: The wood castle playground in the background was built by the teachers and parents of the Amherst community based on the drawings submitted by the Fort River Elementary School children (K to 6).

Walking Calories

Walking and Calories. When you walk, your body burns 5 times more calories than when you *sit*. That is why walking helps you control your weight. However, this does not mean that we can stuff our faces with thousands of extra calories. Consider a shiny red apple. How far would you need to walk to burn it off. A half mile? 1 mile? 2 miles? What about a carrot stick or a stalk of celery?

Walking Off Your Snack Pack In this *Walking Calories* workshop you will be handed a *snack pack* containing 5 food items. For each food item, a team will be named (see chart below). Next, you will be placed on one of these teams. Your team goal is to *walk* just the *right* distance on the *Straw Walk* course to burn off the number of calories contained in your team's food item. Each team will get its turn at *walking off* its own food item.

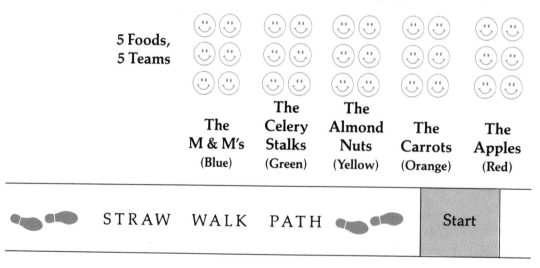

Joining Your Team Huddle with your teammates as shown above. As you are handed your *snack pack* look inside, *but do not eat yet*. Snack time will come shortly. For now simply discuss with your teammates how far you'll need to walk to burn off your team's food item! Remember this is a *team project!*

Note In this workshop it was intended that each of you would: (a) *Receive a snack pack,* (b) *eat the snack pack food items* (one by one), and then, (c) *burn off the food calories by walking.* However, if for whatever reason, you do not feel like eating any or all of the foods in the snack pack, then do not force it. Simply pretend to have eaten the food(s) so you can complete this *Walking Calories* workshop.

Starting the Apple Walk

After everyone has had a chance to bite into their ¼ slice of apple, **The Apple Team** should now begin walking (3.5 MPH pace) around the *Straw Walk* course. As you walk, discuss how far you will need to walk to burn off the ¼ apple section. Stop when you think you have walked off the apple. *For everyone else:* Follow behind **The Apples**. When **The Apples** stop, you should stop too. Do you think **The Apples** walked the right distance? *For everyone:* Turn to the *Walking Calories Chart* on page 36. *First* fill in column 5 by counting how many ¹⁄₁₀ markers you walked. *Next* fill in column 4 by multiplying the *number of tenth markers in column 5* by the number 2. Why by 2? Because as it turns out, you burn 2 calories every time you walk the length of a pair of ¹⁄₁₀ markers. The only question that remains now is: *How many calories were in the ¼ apple?* Listen to your teacher for that answer, and then fill in the correct number under column 3. Compare the calories you *ate* with the calories you *burned.* Did you have a *net gain* or a *net loss* in calories during the *Apple Walk?* _____.

The Carrot Walk

From the point where **The Apple Team** stopped, eat (or pretend to eat) your carrot stick. Then **The Carrot Team** should step forward to lead the way. Now the goal is to walk enough to burn off the carrot stick. When **The Carrots** stop walking, complete the second line of the *Walking Calories Chart.*

The Almond Nut Walk

Repeat the same procedure starting from where **The Carrots** decided to stop walking.

The Celery Stalk Walk

Repeat the same procedure starting from where **The Almond Nuts** decided to stop walking.

The M & M Walk

Repeat the same procedure starting from where **The Celery Stalks** decided to stop walking.

Walking Calories Chart

(1) Walk Description	(2) Food Eaten	(3) Calories Eaten	(4) Calories Burned	(5) Distance Walked (Number of ¹⁄₁₀ Markers)
Apple Walk	¼ apple	_____	_____	_____
Carrot Walk	3″ carrot	_____	_____	_____
Almond Walk	1 almond	_____	_____	_____
Celery Walk	3″ celery	_____	_____	_____
M & M Walk	1 M & M	_____	_____	_____
TOTALS		_____(cal)	_____(cal)	_____(¹⁄₁₀ markers)

Completing the Workshop   After all 5 walks, *add up* column (3), column (4), and column (5) and record your sums on the line labeled TOTALS. Did you eat more calories than you burned off walking? Or did you burn off more calories walking than you ate?

■■■■◄► Homework — Workshop 7

Part (A)   Answer all questions below by circling the best multiple choice answer. Base your answers on this and your previous workshops.

(1) If your snack pack contained 40 calories of food, how many ¹⁄₁₀ markers would you need to walk to burn off your entire snack pack?
 (a) 2   (b) 4   (c) 8   (d) 12   (e) 20

(2) If column (4) totaled more than 40 calories, would you be on your way to *gaining* or *losing* weight?
 (a) gaining   (b) losing   (c) neither

(3) If you burn about 2 calories every time you walk the length of a set of ¹⁄₁₀ markers, how many calories would you burn walking 1 mile (4 laps)?
 (a) 20   (b) 80   (c) 120   (d) 180   (e) 300

(4) How many laps of the *Straw Walk* course would you need to walk to burn off a 400 calorie apple pie and vanilla ice cream dessert?
 (a) 1 lap   (b) 2 laps   (c) 5 laps   (d) 10 laps   (e) 20 laps

(5) One minute of walking burns about 5 calories of food. About how many minutes of walking are required to burn off your *snack packs?*
 (a) 2 min.   (b) 4 min.   (c) 8 min.   (d) 10 min.   (e) 20 min.

Part (B)   Read pages 31–33 to prepare for Workshop 8.

Meal-Walk

Consider **what** you are eating as well as **how much**!

Most fast food chains cook their french fries, chicken and fish in beef tallow** which is very high in saturated fat—the kind of fat associated with high cholesterol levels, plugged and hardened arteries, heart disease and stroke. A 300 calorie portion of french fries, fried chicken, or fried fish could easily be dripping wet with 150 calories of these saturated fats.

Actually you would be better off eating a home-cooked meal of steamed vegetables and salad with broiled fish, poultry or lean beef, than to swallow the fast food tallow.

As Daniel Levy, director at the Framingham Heart Study, said: "For many, fast foods are a way of life—and a way of death."

**Hopefully the fast food industry will change its recipes by cooking with polyunsaturated oil instead of beef tallow in the near future.

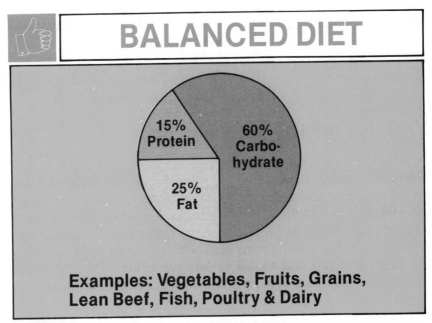

BALANCED DIET

15% Protein
60% Carbo-hydrate
25% Fat

Examples: Vegetables, Fruits, Grains, Lean Beef, Fish, Poultry & Dairy

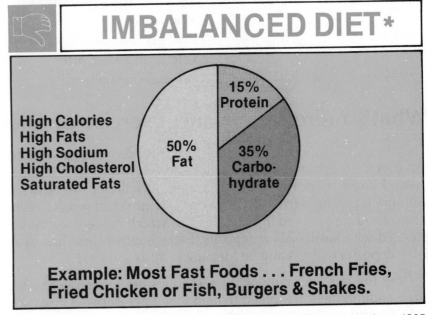

IMBALANCED DIET*

High Calories
High Fats
High Sodium
High Cholesterol
Saturated Fats

50% Fat
15% Protein
35% Carbo-hydrate

Example: Most Fast Foods . . . French Fries, Fried Chicken or Fish, Burgers & Shakes.

*Percentages represent average fried food compositions based on 1985 (and prior) fast food meals.

Meal-Walk

A Review of Walking Calories   In the *Walking Calories* workshop you discovered that walking 1 lap of the *Straw Walk* course burns 10 × 2 or 20 calories. By walking 4 laps (1 mile), you spend about 4 × 20 or 80 calories of energy.

Watch Out for *Fat* Calories!

Besides the *number* of calories, we must watch the *types* of calories we consume. Our bodies need *carbohydrates, protein,* and *fat* to survive. A balanced diet consists of 15% protein, 60% carbohydrates, and 25% fat. Unfortunately, most Americans consume 40% to 50% of their calories as *fats*—fats that build up inside our blood vessels as hardened cholesterol. These deposits can block our blood vessels, cause heart attacks, strokes and high blood pressure. Close to 1 million Americans die each year from these **Cardiovascular Diseases** —diseases of the heart (cardio) and blood vessels (vascular). *What can you do about it?* First, learn the meaning of the Spanish verb **SABER** which means *to know.*

<u>S</u>tay away from fatty foods.
<u>A</u>void tobacco.
<u>B</u>lood pressure—control it!
<u>E</u>xercise and walk often.
<u>R</u>educe excess weight.

What's more Important: Exercise or Diet?

They both are important, but look at it this way. You can exercise your body into great shape, but if you eat improperly, you will lose your health. It does not matter how good of a car you own; if you put poor fuel in the gas tank, it will not run right. The *worst* kind of *fuel* for your *gas tank* is *fast food* fried in animal fat and most *fast foods* in general, including greasy burgers. These foods are loaded in saturated fats which cause your blood vessels to become coated and plugged with hardened fat deposits. Eat enough of these greasy fried foods, and by age 11 some fatty deposits will already be forming in your arteries!

Besides the fats, so many of the fast foods are loaded with *sodium* (also found in table salt). High-sodium diets are linked to high blood pressure—a disease destroying the blood vessels of over *40 million* Americans today. So next time you get a hunger pang, think of your heart as you make your food choice. That *choice is still yours.*

The Right Meal Choice

Again you will be working in teams—the *same teams* as in Workshop 7. Assemble along the *Straw Walk* course as shown below.

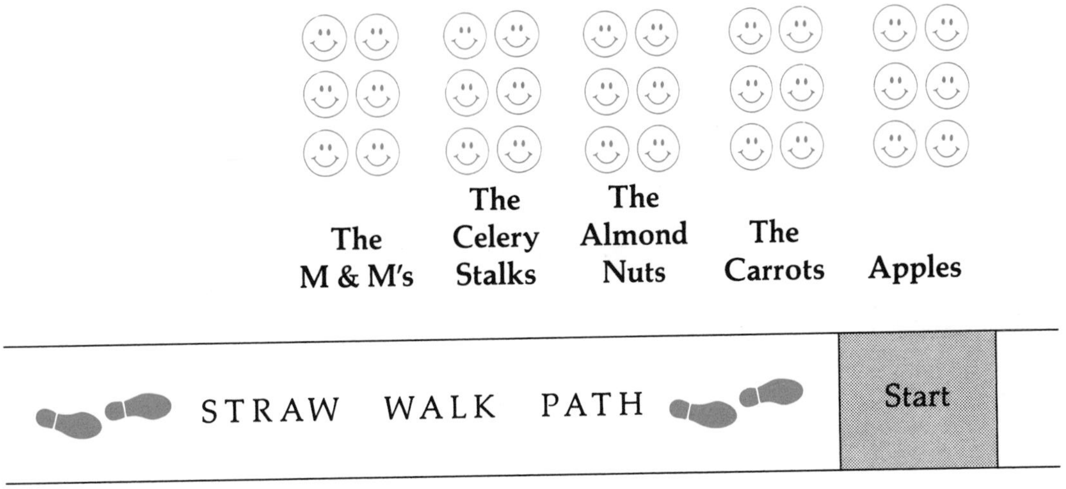

The
M & M's   The
Celery
Stalks   The
Almond
Nuts   The
Carrots   Apples

STRAW   WALK   PATH   Start

In this exercise you will each walk 1 mile (4 laps) on the *Straw Walk* course. During that mile you and your teammates are to pick the *best (healthiest) meal* to *replace the calories you burned while walking.* Your *choices* are shown below.

Choice 1   ⅓ of a Big Mac   Choice 5   ½ cup chocolate milkshake
Choice 2   ⅓ Whopper   Choice 6   1 cup peas, carrots, broccoli
Choice 3   a small french fries   Choice 7   3 fried chicken nuggets
Choice 4   ½ plain baked potato   Choice 8   a fried fish sandwich

Hint Two things you might consider before making your final choice are: (1) **total calories** and (2) **percent fat!**

As you walk discuss each choice, and try to narrow down the field so that by the end of the mile your team has reached agreement on your *best meal.* When you complete your mile, huddle back at the *start line* and *fill in* the chart below. Then be prepared to discuss and defend your team selection.

The Right Meal Choice

Your team name: _____

Your teammates: _____, _____, _____,

_____, _____, _____.

Distance walked: _____ mile(s). Calories spent: _____ calories.

Your team's first choice: _____ Your personal first choice: _____

Why did your team decide on its choice? _____

If by yourself, would you have decided differently? _____

Explain your own reason. _____

Part (A) Carefully study the chart below. Based on this information, answer questions 1 through 5.

Fast Food Nutritional Report Card*

Food Description	Total Calories	Fat Calories	Sodium (milligrams)	Minutes of Walking to Burn off
1. Big Mac	563	295	1010	112
2. Whopper	670	340	975	134
3. French fries	210	100	100	42
4. Baked potato (no topping)	250	17	60	50
5. Chocolate shake	400	120	260	80
6. Raw salad of peas, carrots, broccoli, etc. (1 cup)	80	0	60	16
7. Fried chicken	310	160	700	62
8. Fried fish sandwich	430	222	780	86

*SOURCE: American Council on Science and Health and The Chicago Sun-Times. Based on 1985–86 data.

Question 1
Whether you eat fried chicken, fried fish, burgers or french fries at a typical fast food place, you are eating *poorly* because all of these foods contain:
- (A) Too much fat
- (B) Too much cholesterol
- (C) Too much sodium
- (D) Too many calories
- (E) All of the above

Question 2
To burn off a meal consisting of a Whopper, fries, and a milkshake, you would need to walk for about:
- (A) ½ hour
- (B) 1 hour
- (C) 2 miles
- (D) 4 miles
- (E) 4 hours

Question 3
Which statements below are true?
- (A) Most fried fast food is loaded with fat.
- (B) Fried chicken or fried fish can have more fat than a lean piece of meat.
- (C) Raw vegetables are generally low in fat and sodium.
- (D) Foods high in fat are generally fattening.
- (E) All of the above.

Question 4
To help keep your arteries clean:
- (A) Avoid fried, greasy foods.
- (B) Avoid saturated fats.
- (C) Keep up your walking.
- (D) Avoid tobacco.
- (E) All of the above.

Question 5
Name at least 4 *very fatty, greasy, high-cholesterol foods you would now be willing to cut out of your own diet forever!*

(1) _____ (3) _____ (5) _____

(2) _____ (4) _____ (6) _____

Part (B) Read pages 35–38 to prepare for Workshop 9.

Walking Off Weight

Photo by Patsy Almy.

The Whitney Creek Country Schoolhouse sits in the middle of an open cattle pasture in eastern Montana. When the students go outside to play for morning recess, the cows move out of the schoolyard and the children play. With their teacher, they often walk ¼ mile down a dirt road where they about face at a cattle grate crossing.

Sitting at their lift-top desks in the Whitney Creek Schoolhouse, these students burn up *1* calorie per minute. Walking on this country road, they burn about *5* calories per minute. That is why walking helps you control your weight. Just 15 extra minutes a day of walking can help you lose 7 pounds in a year without dieting!

Pictured are 1st grade: Richard, Scotti and Jeremy; 2nd grade: Melissa; 3rd grade: Tim and Matt; 4th grade: Tom; 5th grade: Robert; 6th grade: Tanya; 7th grade: Melvin; and teacher Ms. Jolene Langin and her 3-year-old Alaskan Malamute dog.

Walking Off Weight

Walking for Weight Control A great way to reduce weight is to *walk*. The longer you walk, the more fat you burn up. Even *easy-walking* burns fat well. In fact if you're overweight, it's better to take *long easy walks* than *short fast walks*, because the *easy walks* will not exhaust you rapidly. Besides, they are safer. However, *very slow walking* can be more tiring than *easy walking*. *Very slow walking* barely burns up enough fat. At a 2 MPH turtle's pace, it would take you 24 hours to walk off a pound of fat. For best results, walk at a *steady, comfortable pace* . . . not too fast, not too slow. Walk between 3½ and 4 MPH.

The Walk-Off-Weight Game

Most of you probably do not need to lose weight, but just for this exercise let's pretend you do—8 pounds worth of weight, in fact. Here's how the *game* works. First you will be assigned to 1 of 3 teams. Each team will be given 8 *straws*. Each *straw* represents 1 of the 8 pounds you need to lose. Each time you and your teammates complete a lap you will have an opportunity to lose *weight* by handing your teacher either 1, 2, or 3 straws. The number of straws you get to shed is based on how fast your team looped the *Straw Walk* course.

The Game:
Walk-Off-Weight

Orange
Team

Yellow
Team

Red
Team

S T R A W   W A L K   C O U R S E   Start Line

Rules of the Game

Case 1 If you walk slower than 3.5 MPH (4:17 lap time), you shed only *1* straw (1 pound) and your team gets to continue walking. **Case 2** If you walk between 3.5 and 4.0 MPH (4:17 to 3:45 lap time) you shed 2 straws (2 pounds) and your team gets to continue walking. **Case 3** If you walk over 4.0 MPH (3:45 lap time) you shed 3 straws (3 pounds). *However*, you will be asked to sit out 1 *whole lap* during which you will gain 1 straw for being inactive. Such sitting will *not* let you reach your 8-straw goal.

Your Walk-Off-Weight Goal

Since your goal is to lose 8 pounds in 4 laps, you and your team need to walk between 3.5 and 4.0 MPH to consistently lose 2 straws (2 pounds) each lap. Funny how in real life it works the same way—slow, steady, consistent weight loss. Remember, if you walk too slow, your team will not lose enough weight. If you walk too fast, you may do well that first lap (minus 3 straws) . . . but you will also be *benched* at the end of that lap. The trick is to walk somewhere between 3.5 and 4.0 MPH. This way you can keep *shedding* 2 straws each lap to reach your goal of losing 8 straws in 4 laps.

Teamwork Do you remember how you and your teammates worked together in the *Teamwalk* (Workshop 4)? That kind of teamwork is critical here, too. So discuss how fast your team should be walking. Once again remove your wrist watches to avoid the temptation of checking your lap time. Your teacher will keep track of time for you. You and your team only need to focus on your *walking pace. (Remember: Your goal is to keep moving and not to be **benched**. If you walk **slower than 3.5 MPH** or **faster than 4.0 MPH**, you will not make your **8 straw** goal.*

Record Your Lap Times

Lap 1   Start time ____:____   Finish time ____:____   Lap time ____:____

Lap 2   Start time ____:____   Finish time ____:____   Lap time ____:____

Lap 3   Start time ____:____   Finish time ____:____   Lap time ____:____

Lap 4   Start time ____:____   Finish time ____:____   Lap time ____:____

Lap times: 4:17 or more . . . Shed 1 straw   3:45 to 4:17 . . . Shed 2 straws
3:45 or less . . . Shed 3 straws, but sit down.

When You Pass Go! As you approach the finish of each lap, listen carefully for your *finish time*. Quickly record your *lap time*. Hand your teacher 1, 2, or 3 straws based on your lap time.

After Your 4th Lap Huddle back at your original team spot and begin discussing your team performance. Answer the questions below.

(1)   How many pounds (or straws) did your team lose? _____

(2)   Did you function well as a team together? _____

(3)   What could you have done better? _____

(4)   What does this lesson prove to you? _____

Homework — Workshop 9

Part A　It takes about *one calorie* per minute of human energy to keep a pair of eyeballs focused on the TV. Unglue yourself from the TV, rise up, start walking, and all of a sudden your body starts burning *five calories* of fuel per minute. That's *400%* more fuel than when sitting! That is why *walking* helps you lose weight.

You need to burn up an extra *3500 calories* of *stored food* to shed *one pound* of *body fat*. For each ½ hour of walking you substitute for TV, you burn up about an extra 120 calories. The average student watches *27 hours* of *TV per week*. How much TV would you be willing to give up in favor of *walking* for your health?

Your homework assignment for this week is to keep a **Walk-Instead-of-TV Log.** This will be your personal journal. The way it works is simple. Every time you substitute **walking** for a **TV show**, you record it below. This way you can tell just how many extra calories of fat you have burned off. Before you start, set a *calorie goal* for the week. Could you give up *3 hours* of TV for *walking* this week? That's a 720 calorie loss or about ⅕ *pound of body fat!*

Your Goal = _____ Calories	Walk-Instead-Of-TV Log		
Day Date	(1) **TV Show Given Up**	(2) **Time Walked Instead of TV**	(3)* **Calorie Difference**
Day 1 __/__/__	_____	_____ minutes	_____ cal.
Day 2 __/__/__	_____	_____ minutes	_____ cal.
Day 3 __/__/__	_____	_____ minutes	_____ cal.
Day 4 __/__/__	_____	_____ minutes	_____ cal.
Day 5 __/__/__	_____	_____ minutes	_____ cal.
Day 6 __/__/__	_____	_____ minutes	_____ cal.
Day 7 __/__/__	_____	_____ minutes	_____ cal.
	Walking Totals =	_____ min. × 4 =	_____ cal.

*To fill in column (3), multiply the number in column (2) by 4. That is *how many more calories* you burn each minute you *walk* instead of *watch TV.*

Did You Make Your Goal? _____ Add up column (3), and compare it to *your goal.* If you keep this up for the year, how many extra calories would you burn in 52 weeks? _____. **Hint:** Multiply your colum (3) total by 52!

Final Question　How many pounds would that be per year? _____.
Hint: Divide total calories by 3500 since there are 3500 calories in 1 pound of stored fat.

Part (B)　Read pages 39–41 to prepare for Workshop 10.

★ ★ ★ **End of Workshop 9** ★ ★ ★

Tobaccoless Road

On the left: An inside view of the clean, healthy artery of an 11-year-old boy who never touched tobacco.

On the right: The same artery (hardened with plaque) in the body of a 50-year-old woman who started smoking early in life.

The main point: Nicotine from cigarettes or chewing tobacco destroys your blood vessel walls.

Question: How will your arteries look 5, 10, or 20 years from now?

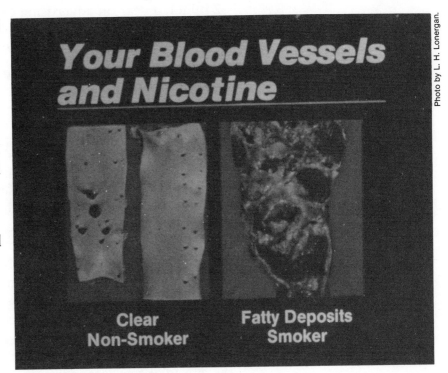

Photo by L. H. Lonergan.

Tobaccoless Road—Part 1

Tobacco—A Killer Tobacco is the biggest *killer* in America. Research now shows that tobacco causes 300,000 American deaths each year! Yet the American tobacco industry still spends $2 Billion a year on advertising to get us to buy a product that causes *heart disease* and *cancer.* Their advertising glamorizes tobacco, but the *real truth* about *tobacco* is proven:

Smoking causes *lung cancer, heart disease, emphysema, and childbirth defects.* Chewing tobacco, also containing tars and nicotine, causes cancer and heart disease.

Think about it: 300,000 dead Americans because of tobacco. Such waste and suffering. Worse yet, tobacco can effect you even if you do not smoke. When you sit in a room filled with stinky tobacco smoke, you breathe the smoker's poisonous air. It contains *carbon monoxide*—the same deadly gas that shoots out of the exhaust pipes of cars and buses. *Carbon monoxide* goes through your lungs and into your blood where it poisons your red blood cells—starving them of *oxygen.* That is why smokers get winded walking up one flight of stairs. By breathing in a smoke-filled room, you can suffer from sore throats, headaches, inflamed eyes, sinus congestion—not to mention the more serious, long-term cancer risk. (Estimates now show that thousands of non-smoking Americans die of lung cancer from the effects of this secondary tobacco smoke). This whole issue goes well beyond the *health of smokers; it affects your health too!*

What You Can Do To Help Yourself

First focus on yourself. If you stay *free of tobacco the rest of your life, you will: (a) have the best chance to stay healthy; (b) help kill the tobacco industry; and (c) set a good example for others.*

Think About This The American Tobacco Industry's only hope for the future is *you.* If *all* the children of America grow up hating tobacco, then who will the tobacco people sell to in the year 2000? No one! That is the point. *You* are in control. *You* can kill tobacco before it kills *you!*
Saving Money Besides, think of all the money you'll save! A pack-a-day smoker spends $20,000 on cigarettes in a lifetime of smoking. If that $20,000 was earning interest in the bank, it would be worth $40,000 in your retirement bank account. What could you do with $40,000? How many smokers do you know that burn up $40,000 in a lifetime to destroy their lungs and hearts?

How Can You Help Someone Else?

About 50 million American adults smoke or chew tobacco. Also, about 50 million children *do not* use tobacco. *Think about this:* What if *every child* could convince just *one adult tobacco-user to quit?* We could free America of our biggest health problem. *Would you be willing to help one person quit tobacco?*

Starting Down Tobaccoless Road How often have you asked a close relative or friend to quit smoking, only to hear them respond, "I'm trying"? In one ear and out the next. Yet the *written word* is different. What if you put your thoughts down on paper in a letter to that person? That would make a much stronger impression because it shows that you are concerned enough to take the extra time to write. Yes, one letter could make the difference!

Writing your Letter Your goal in this workshop is to use walking as an exercise to help you compose thoughts for a letter you will *write* and *deliver* to a tobacco-user as part of your homework. Again, you will work in teams, but each of you will be required to write your own personal letter.* Use your 1-mile team walk to discuss to *whom you want to write*, and *what you want to say*.
*Note: 4 teammates should identify 4 people to whom they want to write. However, if several of you identify the same party, then you can write personal letters to that party.

Hints In choosing a tobacco-user, think about someone you really care about—a relative, a teacher, a good friend. In your letter just be yourself. Be honest. Tell why you are concerned. Try to offer some help. Sincerity is your greatest tool.

Taking Notes

Use the space below to write down your ideas *before* and *after* your *Tobaccoless Road* walk.

(1) List your teammates. _____, _____, _____,

_____, _____, _____, _____.

(2) Who will you write to? _____.

(3) How will you show you care? _____

_____

(4) What would you be willing to do to help that person quit? _____

_____

(5) What good ideas did your teammates mention? _____

_____

Your assignment is to:
(A)   *Write* and *deliver* a letter to your chosen tobacco-user
(B)   *Follow-up* on your letter by making sure you get a *response*
(C)   *Be prepared* to discuss that response in your next workshop

Part (A)

Preparing your letter   Make your letter *neat*. Make it look like you care! Write from your heart. Your sincere words can inspire someone. Consider offering something in exchange for *quitting,* and try to close your letter by asking for a response. Consider this example:

Dear Mother,

   I am so concerned about your smoking and health. I know it is tough to quit, but if you do I'll promise to wash the dinner dishes once a week for the rest of the year. Would you take me up on my offer? Please!

                              Sincerely,
                              your loving daughter

This is just one example. There are all kinds of personal sacrifices you could make to show you really care. Before you seal up your letter for delivery, copy it in the space below for your records.

Dear _____,

_____

_____

_____

Delivering your letter   Try to hand deliver your letter. That way you will know it reached its destination. Consider enclosing a self-addressed return envelope to make it easier for your party to respond to you. Realize that you will need to receive a response within a week, so deliver your letter—the sooner the better!

Part (B)

Follow-up for your response   This may take a little doing on your part. The best way to get a response is to *ask* for one in your letter. In any event, do not hesitate to make a follow-up contact after your party has had a day or two to read your letter.

Part (C)

Preparing for Tobaccoless Road—Part 2   In the space provided below, prepare a brief outline for a short talk you will give to your classmates, and read pages 43—45 (Tobaccoless Road—Part 2).

(1)   To whom did you write? _____.

(2)   Why that person? _____.

(3)   Describe your letter. _____.

(4)   Describe the response you received. _____.

(5)   How do you feel about your efforts? _____.

Tobaccoless Road PART 2

Life is a road full of intersections. Some roads are short and painful. Others are long and pleasurable. Read the road signs well, and have a long, healthy journey . . .
Walking Hawaii by Rob Sweetgall.

On January 28, 1985 I flew to Honolulu to include Hawaii on my 50-state walk. From the airport I walked 8 miles down Nimitz Boulevard to the old fishing pier near downtown Honolulu. An unshaven, hunched fisherman stood on the dock by a tuna boat smoking a cigarette while sipping on a can of beer. I looked into his yellowish red eyes and asked him what he was celebrating. In a raspy voice he answered, "My crew just landed a boat full of tuna in six days at sea." He pulled a piece of paper out of his stained pants. It was a check for his catch . . . $30,000. I looked at his sickly figure and thought, "All the money in the world doesn't mean a thing if you don't have your health." Later I walked down the pier, bought a 50¢ container of white rice, and sat for dinner on some lava rocks, dangling my red feet in the salty, blue-green waters of the Pacific. Some native boys paddled their outrigger canoes through the rolling waves out from the beach's surf. Their wealth was their health.

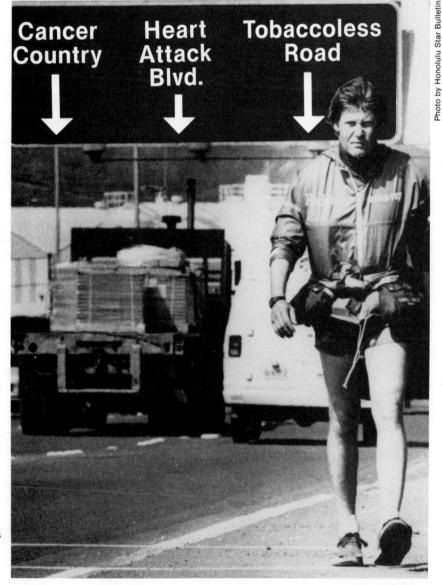

Photo by Honolulu Star Bulletin.

Tobaccoless Road—Part 2

Discussing Your Letters and the Responses They Received In Workshop 10 you used *walking* to generate ideas for your *Tobaccoless Road* project. Now, with the same teammates from Workshop 10, you will have a chance to discuss *the results* of your *letters* on a follow-up walk. This walk will last *only 10 minutes*, so each of you will need to summarize your accomplishments quickly. In speaking to your teammates, focus on answering these questions.

(A) To whom did you write?
(B) What was your approach?
(C) How did you deliver your letter?
(D) How did you follow-up?
(E) What response did you receive?
(F) What did you accomplish?
(G) What did you learn?
(H) What could you do in the future to follow-up on this project?

After Your Team Walk

Regroup with your teammates and summarize the highlights of all of your speeches.

My Teammate's Accomplishments

Teammate's Name: _____ : _____

Teammate's Name: _____ : _____

Teammate's Name: _____ : _____

Teammate's Name: _____ : _____

Teammate's Name: _____ : _____

Teammate's Name: _____ : _____

Teammate's Name: _____ : _____

Elect a Team Spokesperson After five minutes of writing, quickly elect a *team spokesperson* to make a 3-minute speech summarizing your *team's accomplishments.*

Note Your team spokesperson must represent your *total team* by painting a full *picture* of your team's activity.

Listen to How Other Teams Did! As each *team spokesperson* addresses your class, listen attentively to see how they handled this project. Record any ideas that impress you in the space below.

Red team: _____

_____

Orange team: _____

_____

Yellow team: _____

_____

Green team: _____

_____

Blue team: _____

_____

Summarizing Tobaccoless Road

Think what this *Tobaccoless Road* workshop has taught you about (1) *deadly tobacco,* and (2) *writing letters* and *getting people to respond to them.* With this in mind, *what do you think are the most important things that you have learned through Tobaccoless Road Workshops 10 and 11?*

What I Have Learned

_____

_____

_____

_____

_____

_____

▬▬▬▬▬ ► Homework — Workshop 11

Part (A) Answer TRUE or FALSE for each of the statements below.

(1) _____ TRUE _____ FALSE If you are in a room filled with tobacco smoke, then you also receive the harmful effects of that smoke.

(2) _____ TRUE _____ FALSE Besides causing *lung cancer*, tobacco kills hundreds of thousands by damaging blood vessels and the cardiovascular system.

(3) _____ TRUE _____ FALSE Chewing tobacco is not harmful to the body because the chewer does not breathe smoke.

(4) _____ TRUE _____ FALSE If you start smoking or chewing as a teenager, you may never be able to quit because of nicotine addiction.

(5) _____ TRUE _____ FALSE One good reason why it never pays to get started on tobacco is because it can damage your lungs, heart and blood vessels early in your life.

Part (B) List 3 reasons why you should never smoke or chew tobacco in your lifetime.

(1) _____

(2) _____

(3) _____

Part (C) If someone at school walked up to you and asked you to try tobacco, how would you respond?

_____

Explain why you would give that answer.

_____

Part (D) Are you now willing to take the Tobaccoless Road Pledge?

Tobaccoless Road Pledge

For all the reasons stated above, I, wanting to respect my body and live a long and healthy life, do hereby make a personal commitment to my health and the health of my family by promising never to use any tobacco products for the rest of my life.

X _____

(Your Signature)

Part (E) Read pages 47–51 to prepare for Workshop 12.

Your Planet Earth

Crossing the Continental Divide (December 5, 1985): Students from Helena and Anderson Middle Schools in Helena, Montana are getting a spectacular view of the Rocky Mountains as they walk to the top of McDonald's Pass with Rob Sweetgall. Over 6000 feet above sea level you can observe this magnificent mountain range spanning the North American Continent. When the snow caps on these mountains melt, the water flows in 2 directions. The streams trickling down the west slopes of the Rockies will eventually wind up in the Pacific Ocean. The waters running down the east slopes head toward the Atlantic Ocean. What kind of observations of your planet could you make if you crossed the Continental Divide, *or* if you went on a *nature walk* right around your own school neighborhood?

Walking in nature: These Fort River students are exploring *their planet Earth* on a *nature walk* right on their own school grounds. In an age where more and more of our planet is becoming covered with concrete sidewalks and asphalt parking lots, walking gives us the time to respect and appreciate the beautiful earth and vegetation we inherited.

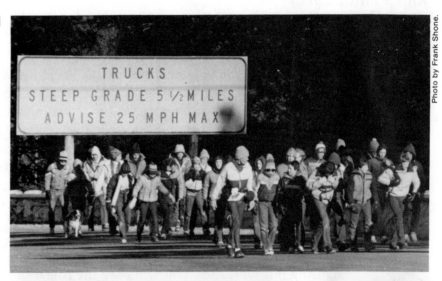

Photo by Frank Shone.

Photo by Joanne Witek.

Your Planet Earth

Walking on Planet Earth   The best way to see something is *on foot*. You notice things walking at 3 miles per hour that often fly by your eye while sitting in a 40 MPH car or bus. Consider your ride home from school. What *details* of *nature* do you remember from all those trips you have taken by car or bus? It is like trying to take a photograph on a spinning merry-go-round. Everything gets blurred. Yet the walker gets to take a slow-motion *snapshot*. The image is captured by the eye and held for a long time. Also, the sounds and smells of nature help you remember that image. These are some reasons why walkers are such great observers.

Being A Walking News Reporter

During this workshop you will play the role of a *walking news reporter*—like a Charles Kuralt "On the Road." In this workshop your main objectives are to: (1) practice your *observation* skills, (2) appreciate your *environment*, (3) practice your *journalism* skills, and (4) appreciate *walking* as a means of discovery.

Getting a Headstart on Your Homework   Your homework assignment will be to write a *short story* on any aspect of this workshop walk you find interesting. For example, consider the topics below.

The Sounds of Nature	Wildlife in My Neighborhood
Appreciating My School Grounds	Things I Never Noticed Before
Pollution in My Environment	How People Behave on a Walk
Walking in Traffic	Life on Main Street
Trash Along the Highway	The Sky Above

Picking a Topic   You do not need to select a topic before your walk. Simply concentrate on everything around you as you walk, and let your *senses* be your guide. In other words, focus on whatever interests you the most!

Where to Walk?   It really does not matter. There are things to see everywhere. You can walk a 1-mile loop around your school grounds, stroll down a country road, or just take a walk down Main Street. Wherever you do go, it will be important for you to stick together as a class.

Taking Notes on the Walk

Every good news reporter takes notes to "jog" the memory. Details are tough to remember unless you write them down. When you write something on paper, it forces you to think a second time. That is how you learn.

To help you take notes on your walk, you will be given a 2-minute break after every 5 minutes of walking. Take advantage of those 2 minutes to write down all the things that impress you: the flowers, the birds, the sky, the trees, the smells, the sounds, etc. *Be as specific as possible,* and *take note of details!* Use the space below for your notes.

Your first notes (on leaving school): _____

_____

_____

Your first 2 minute break:_____

_____

_____

Your second 2 minute break: _____

_____

_____

Your final notes (on returning to school): _____

_____

_____

When You Return To School

You will have a chance to describe your favorite observations to your classmates. Listen carefully to your classmates, and take more notes below. These extra notes will help you write your *short story* for homework.

Additional class notes: _____

_____

_____

_____

Homework — Workshop 12

Part (A) Based on the *observations* and *notes* you made during this week's Workshop 12, write a short story of approximately 100 words. Use the space below.

Your title: ______________________	*Your writing outline.* Before writing your short story think about all the things that went through your mind on your last walk. Outline all your good ideas below. Is there a main theme or subject on which you would want to focus?
	Hint: If you are having a hard time composing your thoughts, go out on a short walk of your own. That might clear your head and help get your writing hand moving!

Be prepared to give a brief summary of your short story to your classmates in your next class.

Part (B) Read pages 51–54 to prepare for Workshop 13.

★ ★ ★ **End of Workshop 12** ★ ★ ★

Dealing With Stress

Photo by Joanne Witek.

One of the best ways to relieve stress is simply to go walking outdoors with some friend(s) who are understanding enough to listen to your story. Sometimes just having someone to talk to can help reassure you that your worries are *not the end of the world* and that *you will survive!*

Dealing With Stress

Being Stressed   Stress can work *two* ways for you. Just the right amount of stress can help you perform well. Consider for example, a final examination. Stress can keep you sharp, answering question after question quickly. Yet if that stress is too great, it can turn you into a nervous wreck, breaking you down. What does this tell us? Basically we need to control stress in our lives so that *it* helps us instead of destroying us. One way to do this is by recognizing those *factors* that stress us the most. Look at the list below. Place a check mark in the space next to the items you worry about the most.

All-Time Worry Checklist

_____ School exams	_____ Financial worries
_____ Family problems	_____ Nuclear war
_____ Concern over physical appearance	_____ Peer pressure
_____ Fear of cancer or another disease	_____ Fear of dying
_____ Dating or social problems	_____ Stagefright
_____ Other_____	_____ Other _____

What Can We Do About Stress?

Point 1   Let's say something is eating away inside of you so much you can hardly think about anything else. Do you ever get that way? If only you could ask yourself: *"What's the worst thing that could happen to me? Really!"* If you honestly answer that question, you may see you've been *"making a mountain out of a molehill."* Just try to realize that you will survive with the most important thing in life: *your health.* Then all your other worries become secondary.

Point 2   Often it pays to talk your problems over with someone you trust—a close relative, a teacher, a guidance counselor, or a friend. Just opening up in conversation with a sympathetic listener can do wonders in relieving tension.

Point 3   Outdoor walking will help you reduce stress because the breeze on your face and the fresh scents of nature remind you that you are alive, and there is so much life out there to enjoy. So why worry? Be glad for all the good things out there you can enjoy, and try to improve on the little things that are not perfect in your life.

Walk Away from Stress   Review your **All-Time Worry Check-list** again. In the space below, write down the 2 biggest worries you have right now.

Worry 1 _____ Worry 2 _____

Splitting into Teams   In this *Dealing with Stress* workshop you will be walking in groups of 3. Do not worry about your pace. Just walk relaxed. The main objective is simply to discuss any worries or concerns that you feel comfortable sharing with your teammates. If at first you feel better as a *listener*, then be just that. You can help your teammates relieve stress by listening and being understanding. Once you see this, you'll probably feel like opening up with some of your own worries or concerns. On this workshop walk do not feel as if you need to come up with a total solution to a problem. Just trying to *understand* your problem or somebody else's problem can help tremendously. So as you walk, relax, enjoy the air and companionship of your teammates. As your walking conversation progresses, keep this *big question* in the back of your mind: *"So what's the worst that can really happen from my problem?"*

Upon Returning to School

Take 5 minutes to summarize what you have learned about (1) *stress in your life*, and (2) *stress in your teammates' lives*.

What bothered you before this walk? _____

_____

How do you look at it now? _____

_____

How did you help your teammates relieve their stress? _____

_____

Sharing Ideas With Your Classmates

After recording your thoughts, feel free to share your feelings on stress with your classmates. Probably many of your classmates have the same worries you do. Just hearing someone else's views can help you see that you're not alone. Use the space below to record good comments by your classmates.

Comments by your classmates:_____

_____

_____

_____

Homework — Workshop 13

Part (A) For homework you are to follow up on your class walk by going on a similar walk with a close friend or relative. Ask someone you feel at ease with. Again, try to focus on any *concerns* or *worries* on your mind. Invite your walking partner to discuss any of his or her concerns. As in class, just try to communicate and understand. Do not worry about the "10 million dollar" solution. Often the solution will come easier than you think! After your walk, briefly answer the questions below.

Question 1   What were the main subjects of your discussion?

_____

_____

Question 2   Who discussed what?

_____

_____

Question 3   Did you realize anything new about "stress" in your life?

_____

_____

Question 4   What is it about walking outdoors with a friend that helps you get rid of stress?

_____

_____

Question 5   Name a few people who you would be comfortable walking and talking with on topics that worry you.

_____, _____, _____, _____, _____.

Question 6   How could you arrange to go out on some relaxing, stress-reducing walks in the near future?

_____

_____

Part (B)   Read pages 55–57 to prepare for Workshop 14.

A Walk Across America

An 11,208 Mile Walk

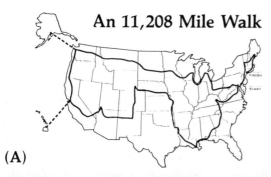

(A)

(B)

Photo by John Gordon.

(C)

(A)   Rob Sweetgall began his walk in Delaware on September 7, 1984, walked straight across the northern Great Plains and Montana's cattle prairie (late autumn) and crossed the Cascade Mountain Range to arrive in Seattle on Christmas Eve. Then Rob walked down the Pacific Coast to San Francisco (January 1985), across the Mojave and Great Basin deserts (mid-winter), along the Colorado River Gorge and back along the Rockies north of Denver. By springtime he was heading downhill, west of the Rockies and across the wheatfields and the cornfields of Nebraska. Rob's summer was spent walking the bayous of Louisiana, the Gulf Coast, and up through the ridge and valley regions of Appalachia before reaching the Atlantic Ocean at Portland, Maine. Rob's homestretch walk was 500 miles through New England. He finished in New York City on Pier 16 on September 5, 1985 completing his 50-state solo walk in 1 day short of a year. What would you pack in a tiny waistpack like the one Rob wore if you were going to walk across America without a support vehicle at your side?

(B)   Rob's feet—20 million footsteps—3 pairs of leather walking shoes slit open with a razor blade for ventilation.

(C)   When you walk across America you can't always pick your days. Some days are warm and sunny; others are wet and sloppy—like day 205 in Colorado Springs.

A Walk Across America

Your New Scholarship   Pretend the American Walking Foundation has just awarded you their "Roads Scholarship." What is a "Roads Scholarship?" Each year the Foundation selects 4 to 6 special students and pays their way on a 4 month walk across America. These students are excused from their fall semester (September to December) for the period of the journey. Yet their education does not suffer. Talented teachers meet the road scholars each day to spend as many as 50 hours a week teaching the students such subjects as: health and exercise, science, geography, environmental science, history, math, reading, and writing.

Let's Make Believe   For the purposes of this workshop suppose a letter addressed to you just arrived in the mail. It reads:

THE AMERICAN WALKING FOUNDATION
2 FOOTSTEP DRIVE
WALKERSVILLE, WY

Dear Roads Scholar Candidate:

Having reviewed thousands of applications, our Foundation is pleased to inform you that you have been selected as one of this year's 30 semi-finalists to *walk across America.*

To help us make our final decision, we are grouping regional semi-finalists in a problem-solving project to test your basic survival and outdoor aptitude and to observe your ability to communicate in a team setting.

The group problem that you will face with your team is to *select from a list of 18 objects the 10 most important ones* necessary for your journey. The specific objects will not be revealed to you until the day of your team meeting next week. However, you can prepare in advance by considering the *most essential* things that you would pack to walk 3000 miles from the Pacific to the Atlantic Ocean, across mountains, deserts and plains, starting in Autumn (September) and ending in Winter (December). You will be hearing from us shortly. Good Luck.

Happy Walking,

Dr. Hugh Will Makit
Dr. Hugh Will Makit

The Semi-Finals   This is it. You and your semi-finalists have been flown to a huge convention center. There, in a conference room, your proctor divides you into 5 teams and hands you each a sealed envelope to open. You open it and read:

> Congratulations on making it to the semi-finals! Listed below are **18** items you may take with you on your walk across America. In selecting your **10**, and only 10 items, assume that there will be a *support vehicle* to accompany you, but that this vehicle has *absolutely* **no** *spare room* to carry extra clothing and articles. Anything you select must be carried on your body by you each and every day of the trip. The support vehicle is heated and equipped with bed bunks, blankets, a completely stocked kitchen, and a bathroom with hot and cold running water. Based on this information, *select* the **10** most essential items you would carry on a 4 month walk across America.

Note   Your team will have 16 minutes of walking to reach its decision. After your team walk, your team will be given a chance to defend its choices.

Hint   To save time, consider ruling out those 8 items you *would leave behind.*

Circle the number of the items you would take:

1. Snowshoes
2. Flashlight
3. Road maps
4. Snake-bite kit
5. Warm mittens
6. Foot-care kit
7. Radio headset
8. Canteen & water
9. Camera and film
10. $1500 in travelers checks
11. $1000 in cash
12. Toothbrush and dental floss
13. Comfortable walking shoes and socks
14. Rainproof jacket and pants
15. Top and bottom wool long johns
16. Waistpack (daypack)
17. Walking journal and pen
18. Insulated, waterproof hat and Hood

Final Team Decision   Darken the numbers of the items you would NOT take with you.

1	2	3	4	5	6	7	8	9	10	11	12	13	14	15	16	17	18

After Your Team Walk   Select a team spokesperson to explain your team choices. Each team spokesperson will have 2 minutes to explain his/her team strategy. Take notes (below) on each team's reasoning.

_____

_____

_____

Part (A)

Your Walk Across America Project

Study the map below carefully, and try to picture yourself starting a journey on foot of the 50 states (Alaska and Hawaii by air). Figure that you will start walking from your hometown at the beginning of the school year-September. In what direction would you head first? Where will you spend the winter? The spring? The summer? Plot your planned course on the map in red pencil alongside of Rob's path. Remember to touch all 50 states in your 1-year walk to bring you back to your hometown by the next school year. Good luck!!!

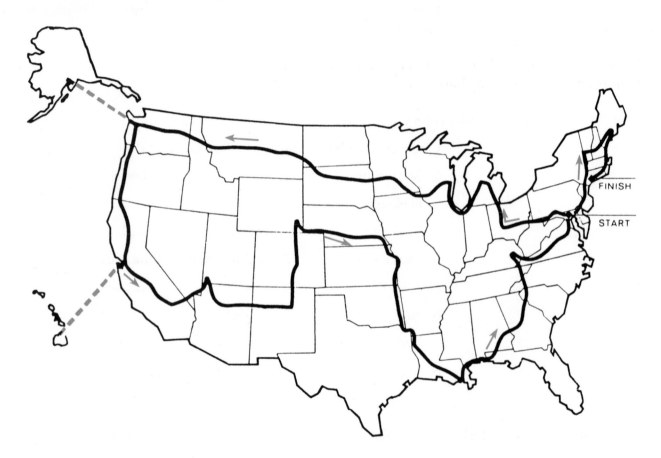

A 50–State Walk

Shown above is the way Rob Sweetgall traveled on his 50–State Walk of America. Rob mapped out his route based on 50-year weather averages to cross Montana before the long, cold winter and arrive in the Mojave Desert at the coldest part of the year–early February. After a winter in the desert, Rob hit the windy Great Plains (springtime), and the Appalachian Mountains and New England's coast by summer. How would you plan a 50-State walk to beat the weather?

Part (B)   Read pages 59–61 to prepare for Workshop 15.

★ ★ ★ **End of Workshop 14** ★ ★ ★

Self-Improvement

Photo by Patsy Almy.

Tree Walks: At the Cottonwood Country School (Ismay, Montana, population 21), the student body of 9 (1st through 6th grade) walks after lunch. They walk to a cottonwood tree that sits precisely 643 yards (6.4 football fields) away from their white wooden schoolhouse on a dirt road along the prairie. Walking to the tree and back to school takes six minutes (at 3.75 MPH). These walks keep everyone alert for their afternoon classes. Pictured are Principal/Teacher: Frank Marble; 2nd grade: Troy, Wendy and Tamara; 3rd grade: Karla; 4th grade: Shawn and Kari; 5th grade: Wade; and 6th grade: David and Jeff.

The Walking Review

What Have You Learned? The purpose of this workshop is to *review* what you have learned through *Walking Wellness* and to see how your body has improved. As you complete each of the following FOUR walking exercises, answer the questions for the particular exercise.

Walking Exercise 1

Assemble at the start of the *Straw Walk* course. Your goal is to walk *1 lap* at a pace of 3.5 MPH. Judge your pace *by yourself—not* by the pace others walk. As you finish, listen for your *lap time.* Then answer questions (1) through (4) below.

1. How close to 3.5 MPH did you just walk? _____ MPH

2. How would you describe 3.5 MPH walking?

    (a) Hardly moving   (c) Brisk
    (b) Comfortable   (d) Exhausting

3. When would you normally choose to walk at 3.5 MPH?

    (a) On a long hike   (c) In everyday walking
    (b) Around school   (d) All of the above

4. If you walked 3.5 MPH for 3 hours, how many miles would you have walked?

    (a) 3   (b) 6.5   (c) 9   (d) 10.5   (e) 12

Walking Exercise 2

Repeat exercise 1 at a 4 MPH pace and answer questions 5 & 6.

5. How close to 4 MPH did you walk? _____MPH

6. How can you distinguish between 3.5 MPH and 4.0 MPH walking?

    (a) At 4 MPH your heart beats faster.
    (b) At 4 MPH you breathe harder.
    (c) At 4 MPH you sweat more.
    (d) All of the above.

Walking Exercise 3

Walk *1 lap* at a pace that will raise your heart rate into the *aerobic target zone* of 120 to 150 *beats per minute*. Check your heart *immediately* after you complete your lap. Then answer questions 8 through 11 below.

8. Did you walk fast enough to raise your heart rate into the aerobic target zone? Answer by circling the appropriate "X".

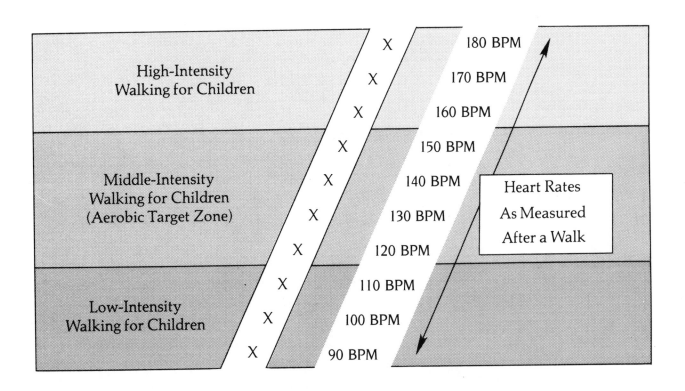

Walking Exercise 4

Your New Straw Walk Score. Remember your first Straw Walk when you tried to walk as many laps as possible in 15 minutes? Turn back to page 12 to review your Straw Walk Scores. Now ask yourself: "Can I top my previous Straw Walk performance?" In this final Straw Walk exercise, try your best to walk as far and as fast as possible in 15 minutes. Record your results below.

My New Straw Walk Record

My first Straw Walk Score _____ . _____ (MPH)   see page 12

My second Straw Walk Score _____ . _____ (MPH)   see page 12

My best score this year _____ . _____ (MPH)

My New Straw Walk Score _____ . _____ (MPH)

Question 1   Compare your New *Straw Walk* Score in Workshop 15 to your past score. If you improved, what made the difference?

_____

Question 2   If you did not improve, what could you still do to increase your walking performance in the future?

_____

Question 3   In this *Straw Walk* you spent enough energy to burn up:

(a) an apple   (b) a celery stick   (c) a carrot   (d) a candy bar

Question 4   In calculating your pulse, why do you count heart beats for 6 seconds and then multiply that count by the number 10?

(a)   10 is a nice number.

(b)   The *Straw Walk* course has 10 sections.

(c)   Since 6 seconds equal $\frac{1}{10}$ minute, we need to multiply our count by 10 to find the number of beats in a full minute.

Question 5   _____ TRUE _____ FALSE   As long as you played sports in your school days, it really *does not* matter if you become inactive later in life.

Question 6   _____ TRUE _____ FALSE   You can completely offset the bad effects of *smoking* and *poor diet* by *exercising*.

Question 7   _____ TRUE _____ FALSE   The best way to stay free of tobacco is to never start using it in the first place.

Question 8   _____ TRUE _____ FALSE   If one of your parents or grandparents had a heart attack, then your health habits are not that important because you will probably have a heart attack anyway.

Question 9   _____ TRUE _____ FALSE   The best reason to exercise is to improve your chances of winning in sports.

Part (B)   Read pages 63–67 to prepare for Workshop 16.

★ ★ ★ **End of Workshop 15** ★ ★ ★

Your New Walking Program

Walking In Wyoming At Pine Bluffs, Wyoming Elementary School all the grades compete against each other for the most miles walked. Here 6th grader, Jesse Curtis, types data (miles walked by the students) into the school computer to keep a record on file of all miles, grade by grade. After some 2300 miles of walking on the Oregon Trail, the 4th grade had built up a 130 mile lead on the 6th grade, and a 400 mile lead on the 5th grade.

A Team Planning Walk

Some of the most creative ideas you will ever think will come to your mind on a walk. In the exercise that follows, you will get a chance to discover this as you walk in teams with your classmates. Your goal is to develop A PERSONAL WALKING PLAN that you intend to follow this summer and next fall. As you walk along with your teammates, discuss all the possible ways that walking could enrich your life. Do not worry about agreeing on a single walking plan. Each of you may well have your own personal preferences. It is much more important for you to develop a plan that is enjoyable for you.

To help you get started, consider a few of the ideas listed below. Check the ones that appeal to you most:

☐ I will walk a mile a day to and from school.

☐ I will walk 2 extra miles for every dinner dessert I eat.

☐ I will help organize a new school walking club.

☐ I will ask my teacher for permission to have our class walk on our free time.

☐ I will take a 10-minute walk at the end of lunch so that I will not fall asleep in class in the afternoon.

☐ I will lose 5 pounds this year by *walking* 15 extra minutes a day in place of watching TV.

☐ I will take short brisk walks to perk me up for my homework when I arrive home from school.

After Your Walk

Take a few minutes to summarize the ideas that you discussed on your walk. Which ones do you think are reasonable for you to follow up on?

Idea 1 _____

Idea 2 _____

Idea 3 _____

Idea 4 _____

Team Discussion

Regroup with your walking teammates and elect a team spokesperson-someone who will give a 3-minute summary of all the ideas that your team discussed on your walk. As a team, prepare an outline to help your spokesperson make an effective presentation. Also, in the space below, take notes on the ideas presented by other teams.

Our Team's Ideas   Other Teams' Ideas

(A) _____   (A) _____
(B) _____   (B) _____
(C) _____   (C) _____

Edward Payson Weston: In 1909, the great walker, Edward Payson Weston, started out from California walking to the east coast. Three months later, he reached New York City. On that walk, Weston averaged 41 miles per day -- at age 71. When he was in his eighties, Weston was still walking 20 to 25 miles per day. How many miles a day would you be willing to walk this summer to stay healthy?

Part (A) In Workshop 16 you listed *your ideas* for making *walking* a greater part of your life. Turn back to those ideas now. Look at them again. Which *ideas* excite you the most? Which idea(s) could you make a regular part of your life?

Your Goal For Homework

Keep developing your ideas for your New *Walking* Program.

Hint 1   A great way to develop your plan is by taking a *walk,* just as you did in school. Take your notebook with you in case an idea *hits* on your walk. Keep reviewing your old ideas (pages 64 and 65). Also review the *Creative Walking Ideas* shown in your appendix (page 73). Spend at least *1 hour* this week *walking, thinking and writing* to develop a good *Action Plan.* Record individual ideas in the space below.

Your favorite walking ideas

Idea 1 _____

Idea 2 _____

Idea 3 _____

Idea 4 _____

Part (B) Using all the *ideas* you generated both in school and at home, write a short composition on *how you plan to use walking in your daily life to stay healthy.* Let this composition be **YOUR** *NEW WALKING* **PROGRAM.**

My New Walking Program

_____

_____

_____

_____

_____

_____

Part (C) For Your Next Class: Be prepared to discuss **YOUR** *NEW WALKING* **PROGRAM** with your classmates in your next **class.**

A Final Note

Although you have finished all 16 workshops in this course, *Walking Wellness does not* need to end here. Remember, you can walk down **Wellness Road** the rest of your life.

Appendix

The long stretches . . . day 139 . . . A Walk Across America . . . Rob Sweetgall walking and thinking and sightseeing along the walnut orchards of Rio Oso, California.

Photo by David Parker, Marysville Appeal Democrat.

Contents

Ten Walking Wellness Tips

 TIP 1 In starting a fitness walking program, take it easy at first. Build up your mileage and speed gradually, month by month by month. Back off when the first sign of soreness or pain sets in during or after a workout.

 TIP 2 Mix it up! Try a variety of workouts consisting of longer, slower walks and shorter, faster walks. Alternate your *hard* (more difficult) workouts, with your *easy* (less difficult) workouts to give your body recovery time.

 TIP 3 For *weight loss*, walk for time—preferably 6 to 7 days a week. Do not worry about speed. For *cardiovascular conditioning*, walk more briskly (over 70% maximum heart rate) about 3 to 4 days a week.

 TIP 4 On *footwear* and *footcare*—wear comfortable fitting shoes (not too tight) designed for walking—shoes that firmly support your feet. Wear thin, clean, dry stretch socks that wick away sweat. Powder your feet to reduce friction. Air your feet often. They need to breathe, too!

 TIP 5 Give yourself time for *warming up* and *cooling down* so as not to shock your system. Slow, easy walking serves as an excellent warm-up and cool down along with static stretching.

 TIP 6 Avoid walking on roads where traffic is a hazard. Parks, playgrounds and walking trail/courses are safest. It is best to walk in a *group* and in *daylight!*

 TIP 7 For high walking performance, swing your arms forward and back at your sides. Keep your body and head straight. Walk tall! Breathe naturally, step briskly and relax!

 TIP 8 For longer endurance walks, aerobic pacing is critical. Do not walk faster than your *speed limit*—your "cruise control" speed. For example, in the *Straw Walk*, your "cruising speed" is the pace you can maintain steadily for 15 full minutes.

 TIP 9 Avoid walking immediately after heavy meals. Give your body time for digestion. Often though, an easy stroll after a light meal is good. Also avoid eating foods rich in (1) fat (greasy/fried), (2) sugar, and (3) salt. Many "fast foods" are full of fat, sugar or salt.

 TIP 10 *For your mind*—to avoid boredom, try keeping your mind occupied with *pleasant* and *exciting thoughts*—your next meal, a movie you will see, your new creative project, or an interesting point of nature around you. Focus on *anything* that takes your mind off those miles and minutes. Even looking for loose change (coins)* on the ground can pass time.

*Rob Sweetgall kept a walking total of the money he found along the highways and in the streets while walking the 50 states. A penny here, a nickel there. After 1 year, he had found $182.82.

The Walking Calories Chart†

Food Item	Total Calories	Minutes Of Walking To Burn Up Calories
		0 15 30 45 60 75 90 105 120 140
water	0	
12 oz. club soda	1	
1 cup lettuce	10	
1 cup raw spinach	15	
sm. cucumber	25	
1 cup string beans	30	
1 cup watermelon	40	
1 cup popcorn	40	
½ canteloupe	50	
1 oatmeal cookie	50	
1 tbs maple syrup	50*	
slice bread	65	
1 orange	75	
1 cup grapes	75	
1 tbs peanut butter	95	
1 fried egg	100	
med. banana	100	
slice American cheese	105	
1 cup orange juice	115	
1 cup apple juice	115	
1 cup cooked peas	115	
slice buttered bread	125	
1 cup hot oatmeal	130	
12 oz. cola	150*	
1 cup wild rice	150	
1 cup whole milk	160	
med. baked potato (plain)	170	
12 oz. beer*	180	
½ cup raisins	210	
slice pizza*	225	
1 cup ice cream*	250	
slice apple pie*	250	
1 choc. candy bar*	250	
lg. french fries*	300	
med. fast food burger*	360	
2 pc. crispy fried chicken*	500	
1 fast food fried fish sand.*	500	
1 slice pie ala mode*	500	
1 extra thick shake*	700	

*Poor diet choice due to either high sugar, high salt (sodium), high fat or alcohol content.

†Caloric values based primarily on USDA Agricultural Handbook Data and American Council on Science & Health Data.

How To Avoid Your First Heart Attack

Heart attacks do not just happen because people grow old. They happen because people abuse their bodies throughout life. The heart attack is only the final blow.

In the early 1950's medical scientists performed autopsies on young American soldiers killed in the Korean War. In examining our soldiers' blood vessels, doctors discovered thick, hardened deposits of cholesterol stuck to the walls of major arteries in 2 out of every 3 of our 18 to 20-year-old boys. At about this time, scientists in Framingham, Massachusetts started a very revealing research study. They began examining thousands of people in Framingham, looking at their smoking, eating and exercise habits . . . year after year after year . . . for 35 years. By 1980, the researchers found that *half* the town's people had suffered from heart attacks or strokes. But what really impressed the researchers was that they could predict the "heart attack victims" just by looking at their lifestyles habits. The victims shared many of the same *risk factors*, since named the *Framingham Risk Factors*.

Framingham Risk Factors For Heart Disease

- Smoking
- High blood pressure
- High cholesterol
- Overweight
- Lack of exercise
- Stress
- Diabetes
- Abnormal heart beat
- Family history*

*Family history is more the inheritance of lifestyle than the inheritance of genes.

Look at these *risk factors*. Do any of these appear in your life or in the lives of members of your family? *The more risk factors you have in your life—the greater your chance of having a heart attack.* Many of the Framingham victims had 2 or more *risk factors*. How many do *you* have?

The good new is that these risk factors are controllable. By following good health habits for life, *you* can minimize your risk of having a heart attack. All you need to do is remember what the *letters* of the Spanish verb *Saber* stand for, and make those *letters* part of your life.

Stay away from fatty foods.
Avoid tobacco.
Blood pressure—control it!
Exercise and walk often.
Reduce excess weight.

Would you be willing to go home and teach the meaning of *Saber* to your family?

Glossary—Walking and Exercise Science

Aerobic Occuring in the presence of oxygen.

Aerobic exercise Any exercise in which muscles work, burning fuel in the presence of sufficient oxygen supplies.

Aerobic target zone The recommended heart rate training level for conditioning usually based on a percentage of the maximum estimated heart rate (typically 60% to 80% of maximum heart rate).

Anaerobic Occuring in the absence of oxygen.

Anaerobic exercise Any exercise in which muscles work intensely for short periods of time with insufficient supplies of oxygen (i.e., winds sprints, 50-yard or 100-yard dashes).

Athlete's foot A fungal infection of the skin of the feet often resulting in fluid-filled blisters and red, dry, scaly, itchy skin. Best prevented by keeping feet and shoes *clean* and *dry*, with frequent *airings*.

Blisters Localized skin irritations (characterized by fluid collection under the skin) resulting from excessive heat build-up and friction. Prevented with comfortable shoes, foot powder, air cooling the feet, and clean, dry socks.

Blood pressure The pressure (force per unit area) exerted by circulating blood on the inside blood vessel walls.

Brisk walking A fast pace of walking (typically 4 MPH or more), sufficient to raise the walker's heart rate into the "aerobic target zone."

Cadence The number of total footsteps (lefts & rights) taken in a minute of walking. Typically a walker's cadence ranges from 100 to 130 footsteps per minute.

Callous A build-up of dead, thickened, dry skin occurring at pressure points where there is excessive rubbing and friction.

Calorie The amount of energy it takes to raise 1 gram of water 1°C

Carbon monoxide An invisible poisonous gas (found in tobacco smoke) that attaches to the blood's hemoglobin to "starve" the smoker of needed oxygen.

Cardiovascular system The heart ("cardio") and its network of blood vessels ("vascular") responsible for circulating oxygen and nutrients to the working muscles.

Cholesterol Fatty substances manufactured by the body to help insulate nerves, build hormones and distribute fat throughout the body. Excessive cholesterol (often resulting from a diet rich in saturated fats) deposits in the arteries, blocking blood flow.

Dehydration Excessive loss of body fluid (water) leading to dizziness, fainting or possibly death. Often caused by lack of fluid (water) replacement during sweat-producing activities.

Emotional stress An uptight feeling in an uncomfortable situation involving worry.

Fitness walking A form of natural walking that helps condition the body.

Frostbite Local freezing of the skin occurring when the skin temperature drops below 32°F. Skin turns numb and ultimately goes from red to waxy-white (like frozen meat). Best prevented by properly insulated outerwear.

Heart rate recovery The return to normal resting heart rate following exercise.

Heel-toe walking   The walker's natural foot motion. For example, the walker's foot lands on the *heel*, rolls over the ball, and pushes off on the *toes*.

Hypothermia   Excessive drop in body temperature (1°F to 2°F) due to rapid heat loss resulting in loss of physical motion and in severe cases—death. Best prevented by properly dressing to stay dry and warm, especially in the head region.

Maximum estimated heart rate (MEHR)   The highest rate at which a person's heart can beat. Estimated by the formula: MEHR = 220 − AGE. For example, for a 12-year-old child, MEHR = 220 − 12 = 208 beats per minute.

Nicotine   A drug found in tobacco which: (1) increases stress on the heart, (2) closes down (constricts) blood vessel openings, (3) raises blood pressure, and (4) damages blood vessel walls.

Overtraining   Excessive physical training in any sport leading to overuse injuries, mental burnout, and overall reduced performance.

Pacing   An exercise technique involving smooth, consistent and rhythmic timing to conserve energy over longer periods of time.

Podiatrist   A doctor specializing in the treatment of foot disorders.

Pronation   An excessive inward rotation of the foot on landing, more typical of people with flat feet (low arch).

Race walking   A specific type of brisk walking that relies on hip swivel and high-energy, quick arm swing for fast body propulsion.

Shin splints   A painful muscle injury in the front leg region about halfway between the knee and ankle resulting from *overuse* and *muscle imbalance.*

Side stitches   Sharp shooting pains in the abdominal area directly under the rib cage—often caused by insufficient warm-up, diaphragm expanding into ribs, or trapped gas after a meal.

Straw Walk   A 15-minute, maximal effort walk in which the walker tries to cover as many laps as possible of the ¼ mile long *Straw Walk* course.

Straw Walk course   An accurately measured ¼ mile (440 yards) walking loop marked in *ten*, 44 yard sections.

Straw Walk score   A measure of aerobic walking capacity and aerobic fitness determined by the total number of ¼ mile laps (with partial fractions) walked in 15 straight minutes.

Stress   The rate of wear and tear on the human body as a result of positive and negative changes.

Stride length   The consistent distance measured between 2 consecutive footsteps—left heel strike to right heel strike.

Target heart rate   The appropriate level at which one's heart should beat during aerobic exercise (measured in beats per minute, BPM). Normal range for aerobic walking for children = 120 to 150 BPM.

Walking posture   The position of the human body while walking.

Wind chill factor   A number that measures the combined effect of *cold temperature* and *wind* on body heat loss.

Creative Walking Ideas

20 Wellness Action Plan Concepts
Based on Simple, Safe, No-Sweat Walking

Walking is so natural and inexpensive that we take it for granted, missing golden opportunities to use it to benefit our health. Here are 20 starter ideas to help make walking a greater part of your everyday life.

1. Start a school walking club to "perk" you up after lunch.

2. Challenge your teachers to a *Straw Walk* tournament as an incentive program for getting in shape.

3. Keep a walking journal, and plot your miles on a map to see if you can walk across (1) your state or (2) America.

4. Design a walking field trip that is educational, and propose it to one of your teachers.

5. Plan a project with your teachers that has the day starting with a 10-minute homeroom walk to sharpen your morning mind for the day ahead.

6. Plan on walking to and from school a few times per week.

7. Plan regular weekend hikes with your family, and get them to say *yes* to specific weekend hiking dates.

8. Continue on *Tobaccoless Road* by trying to get 1 friend or relative *off* tobacco and *onto* walking.

9. Maintain a regular (daily) walking diary/journal to practice your writing and observation skills.

10. Set a weekly goal for *increased* walking, and *decreased* TV, and try to make your goals each week.

11. Start a walking committee with your Parent-Teachers Association to increase walking in the community.

12. With your committee, plan a *family fitness walk* for everyone in your school and community.

13. With your committee, start a project to build a safe and scenic walking path for your school and community.

14. Develop a program that uses walking to clean up your own environment.

15. Design you own personal fitness walking program for the next year of your life.

16. With your fitness walking program, maintain a *food log* to see if your walking is helping to improve your dietary habits.

17. Start a family walking club in which you and your family take regular walks each night after dinner.

18. Develop a routine in which every time you get upset or worried about school exams, you *switch* gears by going for a refreshing, relaxing walk.

19. If you need to lose weight, start a fitness walking logbook in which you record *minutes of walking* and *calories expended* (Hint: figure 5 calories per minute of walking, and 3500 calories per pound of body fat.)

20. Follow-up on *Walking Wellness* by practicing such workshops as *Posture Walk, Straw Walk, Teamwalk, Aerobic Walking,* and *Walking Calories.*

★ ★ ★

73

Great Walking Quotations

"Of all exercises walking is the best."
Thomas Jefferson (1786 Letter)

"The sum of the whole is this: walk and be happy; walk and be healthy. The best way to lengthen out our days is to walk steadily and with a purpose."
Charles Dickens

"If you want to know if your brain is flabby, feel of your legs."
Bruce Barton

"I have two doctors—my left leg and my right leg."
George Trevelyan

"A sound mind in a sound body, is a short but full description of a happy state in this world."
John Locke, *Some Thoughts Concerning Education*

"The first wealth is health."
Ralph Waldo Emerson, *Conduct of Life*

"Life is not merely to be alive, but to be well."
MARTIAL, *Epigrams.*

"Take a two-mile walk every morning before breakfast."
Harry Truman (advice on how to live to be 80, on his 80th birthday)

"Before supper walk a little; after supper do the same."
Erasmus

"We must walk before we run."
George Borrow, *Lavengro*

"I am a slow walker, but I never walk backwards."
Abraham Lincoln

"It is health which is real wealth and not pieces of gold and silver."
Mahatma Gandhi

"Walking would teach people the quality that youngsters find so hard to learn—patience."
Edward Payson Weston

"Every walk is a sort of crusade, preached by some Peter the Hermit in us."
Henry David Thoreau, *Walking*

"Two roads diverged in a wood, and I—
I took the one less traveled by,
And that has made all the difference."
Robert Frost, *The Road Not Taken*

"The [English] literary movement at the end of the 18th century was obviously due in great part, if not mainly, to the renewed practice of walking."
Leslie Stephen, *The Art of Walking*

"For you, as well as I, can open fence doors and walk across America in your own special way. Then we can all discover who our neighbors are."
Rob Sweetgall, *Fitness Walking*

"It is solved by walking."

Latin Proverb